Curriculum in

Designing Curriculum and Instruction for Teaching and Learning in Context

Curriculum in Context

Designing Curriculum and Instruction
for Teaching and Learning in Context

LEIGH CHIARELOTT
Bowling Green State University

WADSWORTH
CENGAGE Learning™

Australia • Brazil • Japan • Korea • Mexico • Singapore • Spain • United Kingdom • United States

WADSWORTH
CENGAGE Learning™

Curriculum in Context: Designing Curriculum and Instruction for Teaching and Learning in Context
Leigh Chiarelott

Publisher: Vicki Knight

Acquisitions Editor: Dan Alpert

Development Editor: Tangelique Williams

Assistant Editor: Jennifer Keever

Editorial Assistant: Larkin Page-Jacobs

Technology Project Manager: Barry Connolly

Marketing Manager: Terra Schultz

Marketing Assistant: Rebecca Weisman

Project Manager, Editorial Production: Katy German

Art Director: Maria Epes

Print Buyer: Lisa Claudeanos

Permissions Editor: Sarah Harkrader

Production Service: Scratchgravel Publishing Services

Copy Editor: Pat Tomkins

Cover Designer: Robin Terra

Cover Image: Digital Vision

Compositor: Cadmus

For product information and technology assistance, contact us at
Cengage Learning Customer & Sales Support, 1-800-354-9706

For permission to use material from this text or product, submit all requests online at **www.cengage.com/permissions**
Further permissions questions can be emailed to
permissionrequest@cengage.com

Library of Congress Control Number: 2005925627

ISBN-13: 978-0-534-59212-7

ISBN-10: 0-534-59212-0

Wadsworth
20 Davis Drive
Belmont, CA 94002
USA

Cengage Learning is a leading provider of customized learning solutions with office locations around the globe, including Singapore, the United Kingdom, Australia, Mexico, Brazil, and Japan. Locate your local office at **www.cengage.com/global**

Cengage Learning products are represented in Canada by Nelson Education, Ltd.

To learn more about Wadsworth, visit **www.cengage.com/wadsworth**

Purchase any of our products at your local college store or at our preferred online store **www.cengagebrain.com**

Printed in the United States of America
3 4 5 6 7   23 22 21 20 19

*To my grandsons, Alexander and Zachary,
and to the educators who will shape their lives*

Contents

Preface

Curriculum in Context: Designing Curriculum and Instruction for Teaching and Learning in Context is a guidebook for teachers, curriculum designers, and instructors who teach curriculum design and/or instructional design to undergraduate and graduate students. As such, it provides a user-friendly approach to writing a curriculum for use in pre-K-12 classrooms and in postsecondary settings. Other books on the market are designed to do the same thing, however, so how does Curriculum in Context differ from them?

First, Curriculum in Context takes basic concepts and principles of contextual teaching and learning (CTL) and places them in a historical and philosophical perspective. By presenting these foundational elements of CTL, the text demonstrates that although these elements are not particularly new, they have not yet been fully applied to the basic principles of curriculum and instructional design and vice versa. Many of the excellent resources on CTL available in printed material and on websites are listed in the text. Note, however, that Curriculum in Context is not designed to provide definitive coverage of all aspects of CTL.

Second, Curriculum in Context is primarily a text on curriculum design and instructional design and not a synoptic text on curriculum history, curriculum development, or the politics of curriculum change. Although the text may allude to these topics, it is assumed that the reader has a minimal understanding of these issues either through a synoptic course on curriculum, through experience as an educator, or preferably both. This book could even be considered as a companion or subsequent text in a fundamentals of curriculum course.

Third, *Curriculum in Context* fundamentally holds a Deweyan orientation toward both curriculum design and instructional design. Hence, it is connected to contextual teaching and learning. In this text, as in Dewey's work, concepts, skills, and beliefs need a context to make them meaningful and useful. Similarly, context needs concepts, skills, and beliefs to make experience understandable and to facilitate the construction of knowledge. The approach to instructional design in this text builds on the connection of concepts to contexts as presented through the curriculum design model in Chapter 4. Instructional design stresses the need to connect behavioral approaches to teaching and learning with constructivist approaches. As a result, both the curriculum and instructional design models used in this text seek to achieve the balance and the connection between concept and context, knowledge and experience as exemplified by Dewey in virtually all of his curricular theory and practice.

Fourth, *Curriculum in Context* incorporates an eclectic approach to the practice of designing curriculum and instruction by combining the best work of traditional and contemporary writers and researchers in the areas of curriculum and instructional design. Ralph Tyler's work is juxtaposed with Grant Wiggins and Jay McTighe, Benjamin Bloom with George Posner and Alan Rudnitsky, Robert Gagné and Leslie Briggs with Bruce Joyce, Marsha Weil, and Emily Calhoun. The important contributions of Fenwick English's concept of curriculum mapping is expanded upon by the work of Heidi Hayes Jacobs in helping curriculum designers gather data to inform their decision making. English's more recent work with curriculum audits and curriculum alignment also contributes to the analysis of curriculum data. By juxtaposing these traditional and contemporary influences, *Curriculum in Context* seeks to avoid the often ahistorical approach of curriculum workers whose designs are more politically motivated than they are educationally informed.

Finally, *Curriculum in Context* uses practical examples drawn from the real work of pre-K-12 and postsecondary educators as they design curriculum and write instructional units. In the Appendixes, examples are provided to show how CTL principles and curriculum and instructional design principles are applied to create a curriculum in context. Through the examples, it becomes clear that educators can and do make the important connection between curriculum and the context of the learner. This becomes crucial as the increased pressure to measure and standardize outcomes both statewide and nationally also increases the tendency to decontextualize student learning within the classroom.

At first, *Curriculum in Context* may appear to offer a "cookbook" approach to designing curriculum and planning instruction. However, the purpose of the text is to provide teachers and administrators with the concepts and skills necessary to make curricular and instructional decisions appropriate to their schools and classrooms. This requires them to apply the concepts and skills in this text to their particular contexts. As much as possible, *Curriculum in Context* tries to take them through the processes they will be using as they create their own designs and/or take the responsibility in their schools for curriculum and instructional leadership. Thus, what appears to resemble a cookbook is really the development of an experiential base that can be transferred to an individual classroom or an entire school.

This approach requires the instructor of the course using *Curriculum in Context* to continually place teachers and administrators in small, diverse, ongoing groups in which each component in the design and planning process is articulated, critiqued, revised, and then ultimately connected with all other components. This step-by-step model will enable each group member to experience the process by which curriculum changes are articulated, critiqued, explained, and defended to other teachers, administrators, board members, parents, and students.

The text then leads individual group members into the process of instructional design by connecting the curriculum design product to their instructional design process. Instructional designs emerge from the work done in the curriculum to identify key outcomes, organize outcomes into units or subunits, create maps of essential concepts and skills, and assess the overall effectiveness of the design. Using principles of learning and effective teaching derived from both behaviorist and constructivist philosophies, the instructional design process enables the group members to create learning environments that result in meaningful, contextual experiences for the students.

Alternative unit and lesson design structures for basic lesson plans and plans specific to problem-based learning, project-based learning, service learning, cooperative learning, and the 5-E model connect research and best practices in effective teaching. Selected models of teaching then contextualize the instructional design process by creating holistic learning environments. After each group member completes the instructional design, the design should be presented to other group members to demonstrate how the instructional design evolved from the curriculum design and how the instructional design represents the connection of theory and research to best practices in effective teaching and meaningful learning. Through this structure, the group members will discover how curriculum and instructional design are always contextual.

Acknowledgments

I thank the following reviewers for their comments in the early stages of this manuscript: Kathy Adams, Wright State University; Eugene Bartoo, University of Tennessee, Chattanooga; Sally Blake, University of Texas at El Paso; Janet Buckenmeyer, Lourdes College; Cecil Carter, Florida Gulf Coast University; David Davison, Montana State University, Billings; Richard Diem, University of Texas, San Antonio; William Dunlap, University of Wisconsin, Eau Claire; Susan Etheredge, Smith College; Jan L. H. Frank, St. Cloud State University; Jim E. Hill, California State University, San Bernardino; Corey Lock, University of North Carolina, Charlotte; Kathryn Loncar, University of Missouri, Kansas City; Helena Mariella-Walrond, Bethune-Cookman College; Daniel G. Mulcahy, Central Connecticut State University; Merrill Oaks, Washington State University; Susan Schramm-Pate, University of South Carolina; Mindy Sloan, University of Illinois, Springfield; David A. Squires, Southern Connecticut State University; Eileen Sullivan, Boston University; Brenda Walling, East Central University; Nancy Wiggers, University of Mississippi; and Marsha Zenanko, Jacksonville State University.

I would also like to acknowledge the contributions of the teachers whose work serves as exemplars of contextual curriculum and instructional design. The designs of Julie Ford, Nathan Ash, and Katie Ryan that appear in Appendixes A and B provide excellent models for curriculum and instructional designers to follow. I am also deeply appreciative of Dave Schwan and Lee Floro-Thompson in Bowling Green State University's Instructional Media Services area for their artwork that illustrates Julie Ford's instructional design in Appendix B. I gratefully acknowledge the work of two individuals who helped perform the important tasks of doing background research for the book. Cathleen Samiec provided the essential research material that was needed to begin this project in 2002, and Megan Stitzlein provided the key information necessary to complete the project successfully in 2004. I can't thank them enough. Without question, my most profound gratitude is extended to the Word Processing Center in the College of Education and Human Development at BGSU, and in particular the skills of Judy Maxey and Sherry Haskins, without whom this project would have literally been impossible. Their ability to turn handwritten material into a workable manuscript was phenomenal. They are truly miracle workers.

Finally, I would be remiss if I didn't thank my family for all their support during this long process. They inspire my work and my life.

Curriculum Design
for Contextual Teaching
and Learning

1

❧

Why Design Curriculum and Instruction for Contextual Teaching and Learning?

Educators are currently struggling to maintain control over curriculum and instructional decisions that are increasingly being dictated by national and state standards, proficiency tests and prepackaged, scripted textbooks, programs, and instructional materials. In California, for example, there are 3,500 specific content standard statements across the four major content areas, and these specific statements largely dictate the content that students are expected to learn. In large or influential textbook adoption states, such as California, Texas, Florida, and North Carolina, politically appointed centralized committees determine which textbooks or series local schools can use. These states heavily influence what content publishers put in the textbooks because the adoption of one reading series in *one* of these states, for example, could mean as much as $100 million in sales for a textbook publisher.

In this environment of state centralized control, state and nationally dictated standards, and politically influenced curriculum decisions, educators may question whether they have any role in the design of curriculum and instruction or whether they are simply to deliver predetermined, dictated content set by organizations, committees, and companies beyond their control. Added to this sense of dependence on centralized authorities is the reality of accountability mandated by such legislation as "No Child Left Behind" and state adopted examinations created by for-profit testing services and corporations.

If the teacher's role in the learning process is to be more than a mere conduit of bits and bytes of information, what should that role be? As a potential designer of curriculum and instruction, the teacher in a contextual learning environment plays a role quite different from the scenario just described. A teacher in a learning environment that supports contextual teaching and learning (CTL) has a significant role in the design of curriculum and instruction because ultimately even prepackaged, standardized, scripted, and externally dictated content has to be put into context for the student if any significant, meaningful learning is going to occur.

From the curriculum design perspective, educators will either be making *macro* or *micro* decisions about design, but the design *process* will be virtually the same whether at the micro- or the macro-level. The design process will be explored in more detail in Chapter 3, but important decisions need to be made before creating the actual curriculum design. First, the designer must become knowledgeable about the context within which the CTL design will be created. This means identifying the characteristics of a CTL environment to determine if a curriculum design or redesign is appropriate or desirable. The designer needs to briefly review the historical and philosophical base of CTL. Second, the designer must decide whether macroanalysis and/or microanalysis of the learning environment is appropriate and necessary before beginning the design or redesign. A macroanalysis would involve examining the entire curriculum at a district, program, or grade level. This would include using a *curriculum audit,* which would analyze, through some external agency or consultant, the strengths and weaknesses of the entire system at the desired level. Issues regarding the viability of the *curriculum alignment* for the district, programmatic, or grade level curriculum could also be examined through this process. At both the macro- and microanalysis level, *curriculum mapping* would determine the degree of emphasis of key concepts and skills and curriculum priorities present in the existing curriculum and presumably lay the groundwork for recalibrating those emphases and priorities. Finally, after establishing the need for change, the designer would pose a set of essential questions to guide the design or redesign process. These questions would focus on the extent to which a CTL-based design was possible and desirable, the viability of the existing design and which elements should be retained or changed, and whether the designer has the resources necessary to make the needed changes.

To assist the designer in becoming more knowledgeable about contextual teaching and learning, the following sections will examine the conceptual, historical, and philosophical bases of CTL to assist in the macro- and microanalysis of design. This section then describes the concept and purpose of a curriculum audit, the importance of and necessity for curriculum alignment, and the process and procedures used in a curriculum mapping. Following this examination, the designer will generate essential questions needed to guide the curriculum design or redesign.

THE CONCEPTUAL, HISTORICAL, AND PHILOSOPHICAL BASE FOR CTL

Curriculum does not operate in a vacuum nor is it an abstraction that can be imposed on any learning environment. Curriculum development and are contextual and operates within specific learning environments. Similarly, contextual teaching and learning (CTL) assumes that, by definition, teaching and learning are context driven (Howey, 1998, p. 19) and sees learning environments as existing both within and outside the school setting. However, CTL as a conceptual construct guides the design of curriculum by focusing attention on the importance of both macro- and micro-design contexts. Although the label "contextual teaching and learning" is fairly new, the concept of context has influenced curriculum design for more than a century.

CTL has powerful, deep roots in progressive education, constructivist theory and practice, and problem-based/project-based learning. All of these are indebted to the work of John Dewey as the philosophical and educational precursor of CTL because the roots of CTL are situated within Dewey's work as well as the work of progressive educators in general. This background information facilitates the assessment of the need to redesign or create a new design for the program, course, subject area, or unit in an existing curriculum as a proposed CTL curriculum.

One of the challenges teachers face on a daily basis is making learning relevant to the learners. Students constantly ask, "Why do we need to learn this?" or "Why are we doing this?" and even "What good is this going to do me after this class?" On occasion, teachers struggle to identify why a particular content needs to be taught or learned. Too often, the answer is either (a) it's in the course of study; (b) the national or state standards require it; (c) it's on the state proficiency test; or, worst of all, (d) it's in the book.

Contextual teaching and learning addresses such questions and answers by challenging some basic, traditional assumptions about how content is selected, organized, and delivered. In so doing, it changes the framework from which curriculum and instructional design have historically been viewed. But what is CTL, what are its philosophical and historical roots, and how does it differ from the way teachers have typically constructed classroom learning environments?

What Is CTL?

Perhaps the most widely recognized definition of contextual teaching and learning was developed through a national project funded through the U.S. Department of Education's Office of Vocational and Adult Education and the National School-to-Work Office. This project defined CTL as:

> . . . a conception of teaching and learning that helps teachers relate subject matter content to real world situations and motivates students to make connections between knowledge and its applications to their lives as family members, citizens, and workers. . . . (Berns & Erickson, 2001)

Berns and Erickson suggest that CTL incorporates such strategies as problem-solving, self-directed learning, learning from peers, learning in real situations, and authentic assessment. CTL brings together a variety of contemporary and traditional teaching strategies and learning principles that could probably be traced back to medieval apprenticeships and Socratic teachings, but its primary source appears to be the philosophy and practice of progressive education, Piagetian developmental theory, constructivist principles of learning, and research on effective teaching. As such, CTL does not represent a totally new approach to teaching and learning but rather a system that connects disparate but related approaches that emphasize the following characteristics:

1. Connecting content to learners' experiences
2. Engaging students in active learning
3. Enabling students to have some opportunities to direct their own learning
4. Encouraging the construction of personal meanings from individual and collective experiences
5. Assessing the attainment of outcomes within an authentic situation and allowing for the interpretation of multiple meanings from a single experience
6. Identifying contexts that are appropriate developmentally to the learner

These characteristics provide the conceptual base for contextual teaching and learning and help define it, but how solid is this base from a philosophical and historical perspective? To what extent does CTL represent an updated version of progressive education in theory and practice and to what extent does it diverge from progressivism?

Historical and Philosophical Roots of CTL

Given the definition of contextual teaching and learning, any learning experiences connected to "real world" activities (for example, apprenticeships) or drawn from learners' experiences (Socratic questioning) could be the historical base for CTL. However, when CTL is put in practice, its historical roots are firmly entrenched in progressive education. As noted in *School: The Story of American Public Education* (Mondale & Patton, 2001), progressive educators from Francis Parker to John Dewey to William Wirt were interested in teaching and learning that was based in the experiences of children and connected to the real world around them (pp. 76–77, 86–91).

When Colonel Francis Parker became superintendent of the Quincy (MA) schools in 1875, he put into practice one of the most contextual curriculums of the time and encouraged his teachers to incorporate experience-based activities in each of the major content areas year by year (Katz, 1973, pp. 72–81). Students learned math through solving actual arithmetic problems they would encounter every day. Rather than memorizing rules of grammar, students developed reading and literacy skills through an early form of whole language teaching. Geography skills were developed by working with locations familiar to the students instead of studying distant sites the students had never encountered. School attendance increased and test scores rose dramatically as compared with past performance and with the scores of other schools in the county (Katz, 1973). In the early days of progressive education, Parker showed how crucial contextual experiences are to student learning.

Similarly, John Dewey's Laboratory School at the University of Chicago also put into practice his beliefs about the child and the curriculum (Dewey, 1902). His well-documented curriculum (Cremin, 1964) clearly showed the critical linkage between the experiences of the learner and the collective experiences of humans as depicted in the subject matter being studied. Although frequently criticized as

---

If You Want to Learn More About Contextual Teaching and Learning

The following sites are excellent resources for more information on the theory and practice of CTL. If you are unfamiliar with CTL, consult a selection of these resources before you begin writing a CTL curriculum design.

1. www.ateec.org/curric/ctl/ic.cfm
2. www.usatodayeducation.com/osu/osu.htm
3. www.texascollaborative.org/WhatIsCTL.htm
4. http://jwilson.coe.uga.edu/CTL/CTL.intro/theory.html
5. www.worldwidenews.net/kabob/ct12.htm
6. www.uaa.Alaska.edu/cte/ctl%20proposal.doc
7. www.ncsl.org/programs/employ/contextlearn.htm
8. www.Kennesaw.edu/English/contextuallearning/index.htm
9. http://soe.csusb.edu/jscarcella/stc/ activities.html
10. www.bgsu.edu/ctl/navigation/index.html
11. www.cew.wisc.edu/teachnet
12. www.terc.edu
13. www.horizonshelper.org/contextual/contextual.htm
14. www.cord.org
15. www.ed.gov/inits/teachers/exemplarypractices#context

---

being overly child centered by revisionist historians such as Arthur Bestor (Mondale & Patton, 2001, pp. 114–118), Dewey was a much stronger advocate of the importance of content in the curriculum than many of his contemporaries were. As with present-day advocates of CTL, Dewey (1938) argued strongly that learning emerges from experience, and one's interpretation of experience is always contextual.

William Wirt's Gary Plan (Mondale & Patton, 2001, pp. 86–91) actually created a "mini-society" in the school and brought the local community into the buildings on a regular basis at night and on the weekends. Students learned content through the experiences involved in running and maintaining the schools. In a sense, the school became the center of the community and enabled children, their parents, and their neighbors to address the problems of the community. The school curriculum was the vehicle through which the problems were solved.

Through the work of Parker, Dewey, Wirt, and many other progressive educators, the historical and philosophical base for the curricular practices advocated through contextual teaching and learning is evident. Such practices as service learning, project methods, authentic assessment, problem-based learning, and self-directed learning can all be traced to progressive education.

Although the historical and philosophical base of contextual teaching and learning suggests that the notion of context is central to the design of curriculum, this has not necessarily been the case since the fractionalization and decline of progressivism in the 1930s and its ultimate demise in the mid-1950s with the launching of *Sputnik*. Since that time, content, not context, has been the driving force behind curriculum and instructional design, and it is only since the early 1980s that the assessment of curricular contexts through curriculum audits, curriculum mapping, and ultimately curriculum alignment has emerged to guide the design process. By assessing both the macro- and micro-design contexts, these practices allow curriculum decision makers to connect *content* with *context*.

The Curriculum Audit

The curriculum audit is a macro-design procedure that requires a school or school district to determine the extent to which it is doing what it is supposed to be doing (English, 2000, p. 116). Although a curriculum audit is not the same as an accreditation, it does use a standards-based approach to conduct the audit (p. 116). A school or school district can do an external or an internal audit, and both have their benefits and their liabilities. As Fenwick English notes, whether an audit is done externally or internally, the following facts pertain:

1. Auditors have to be trained to engage in the process.
2. Audits take time.
3. Audits cost money, whether to pay staff from outside the system or to provide compensated time for staff inside the system.
4. Audits contain some political risks for key decision makers in the system (English, pp. 94–95).

The curriculum audit assesses the context in which the existing curriculum design is operating and helps determine if there are systemic variables that either enhance or inhibit the likelihood that curricular goals and objectives will be met. As English points out, an audit works from several assumptions that must be accepted if the audit is going to be successful:

- *Assumption One:* Organizational control is a necessary part of effective design and delivery of curriculum.
- *Assumption Two:* Curriculum is purposive, created by design, and therefore reproducible.
- *Assumption Three:* There are generally accepted ideas regarding curriculum design and delivery.
- *Assumption Four:* The unit of analysis is the school or the school system.
- *Assumption Five:* School systems are rational entities (English, pp. 99–106).

English's analysis of these five assumptions details why he believes that an audit follows a logical process that can be described and articulated so that a school or district can see exactly where the curriculum design is succeeding or failing and thus determine which actions need to be taken to redesign and/or restructure the curriculum that has been implemented and taught. This type of contextual analysis should provide the school's curriculum decision makers with a "big picture" perspective of the macro-design problems they are facing. Although the purpose of this discussion on curriculum auditing is to highlight its importance for establishing a macro-design context, space does not permit an extensive description of the complexities of doing an audit. Fenwick English's book *Deciding What to Teach and Test: Developing, Aligning, and Auditing the Curriculum* (English, 2000) is an excellent resource and starting point for considering whether an audit would be appropriate and purposeful for the particular curriculum design or redesign problem being considered.

Besides or in addition to a curriculum audit, the designer might find it useful to conduct a curriculum mapping to assess the extent to which the advertised curriculum is actually being taught, what curriculum priorities are being emphasized, and what gaps or omissions exist in the curriculum as teachers are delivering it. This curriculum mapping process will indicate the real design context as the classroom teachers in the system perceive and practice it.

Curriculum Mapping

Curriculum mapping is a valuable tool for educators who want to analyze the discrepancy between the planned, advertised curriculum and the curriculum actually being delivered by teachers in the classroom. When Fenwick English introduced the concept of curriculum mapping in the late 1970s, the process largely depended on the input of classroom teachers as they identified the outcomes, topics, concepts, and assessment strategies that they used to represent the curriculum being taught in the classroom (English, 1978, pp. 26–27). English felt that while this type of curriculum mapping was helpful to identify micro-design problems, there were also concerns about the degree of accuracy and objectivity in the teachers' self-reports. He believed that teachers might be tempted to report what they *thought* should be on the curriculum map rather than what they were actually covering and assessing (English, pp. 27–28). One would expect in this era of high stakes testing and legislation such as "No Child Left Behind" that the temptation to report what the standards indicate, what the curriculum guide states, or what the proficiency tests cover would be even greater. English also found that teachers could have misperceptions regarding the amount of time spent on topics or that they might have difficulty describing their own work in terms that were clear and undistorted (English, p. 29). Finally, the entire process could be time consuming for the teacher and require additional in-service training (p. 29). However, English still believes that curriculum mapping can provide important information to the curriculum designer if the process is done effectively and regarded as a positive rather than a punitive exercise.

By 1997, curriculum specialists such as Heidi Hayes Jacobs had developed curriculum mapping to the point where many of English's concerns became less of an issue. For example, the computer technology available today has made the process less time consuming and more accurate for teachers (Jacobs, 1997, p. 7). Jacobs expanded on English's original model by creating a "calendar based" mapping model that stressed both micro (classroom level) and macro (school of district level) mapping (Jacobs, p 3). Jacobs' macro-level mapping resembles English's "vertical" curriculum map that lays out the K–12 curriculum for each content area (English, 1978, p. 31).

To compare and contrast English's and Jacobs's approaches to curriculum mapping, Figure 1.1 illustrates how key concepts and topics in a K–12 curriculum would be depicted following English's vertical mapping process, while Figure 1.2 shows how a kindergarten curriculum would be mapped out using Jacob's calendar-based map.

CONTENT DEFINITION AND SCOPE (describe generally what you teach by topics or subtopics)	
CONTENT VARIATIONS/INTERACTIONS (describe the major variations and interactions that are expected to occur or have occurred)	
EXPECTED OR ACTUAL OUTCOME AND ELAPSED TIME (describe the expected or actual outcomes obtained—you may use the categorization of cognitive, affective, or psychomotor if desired)	
METHODS OF ASSESSMENT/ CORRELATION TO CURRENT SCHOOL/DISTRICT TESTING PROGRAM (describe the degree to which the outcomes are assessed under the current school or system testing program)	
TEXTUAL AND OTHER MATERIALS USED AS TEACHING TOOLS (describe the major text and other significant references used)	

Teacher _____   School _____

Grade _____   Subject _____

FIGURE 1.1 Classroom Curriculum Mapping Worksheet

Source: English (1978), p. 28.

Whether one follows the more basic mapping example created by English or the more extensive calendar mapping example developed by Jacobs, the fundamental structure should still use the key elements identified by English in his original description of a curriculum map. These include:

- Content definition and scope (for example, major concepts, skills, topics)
- Variations to the content that occur during instruction
- Expected or actual outcomes and the time allotted to those outcomes
- Methods of assessment
- Textual and/or instructional materials

The major purpose behind curriculum mapping is to articulate, vertically and horizontally, the major concepts, skills, attitudes, and values and link them to the goals and objectives of the curriculum either on a micro-level (classroom) or a macro-level (school or district). These will then be correlated with the means of formative (classroom-based) evaluation and summative (school/school district)

Integrated Topics	September	October	November	December	January	February	March	April	May	June
Opening Meeting/ Group Dismissal	About Me --	→	(Crossties Finger Plays School Search	i.e., Grand Poetry	Central) – Counting	- Daily – Alphabet	Planning - Dressing Joke-Telling	- Calendar - Choral Unit	Weather Speaking	→
Language Arts/Reading Readiness	Visual - Following Autumn:	----Same Discrim. Directions - "W" Leaves --	Holiday,- Different,- - Visual - Left Questions - Poetry -	Alphabet Sequencing, Imagery To Right Experience ---- Winter	Rhymes - Dot-to-Dot, - Letter Progression Charts, Stories Snow -----	Fine Motor – Listening Recognition - Top- Bottom - Scribble	Opposites – Comprehension – Appreciation Progression Writing Spring:	Classification Beginning of Literature Answering- Beginnings-	Sounds-----	→
Math/ Number Readiness		Counting/	Recognition -----Unifix -----Geo- Shapes	#'s 0-10 → Cubes, Pattern Boards – Sorting	Blocks, Problem Patterning	Counting/ Ordinal #'s Solving Sheets Sequencing	Recognition #'s - Colors Dot-to-Dot	0-100		→
Gametime/ Music/ Rhythms/ Physical Activities			-- Games – Fitness -	Individual Dramatization Rhythm	Skills – Gross Melody – Winter Games	Instruments- Motor Skills				→
Science/ Social Studies/ Health & Safety	---------- Fall	Fire Topics ----- -- Textures	Prevention Nutr'tion - - Map Skills	←-- Winter Safety - Environ. Family- ---- Tri-Town	Topics ---→ Temperature Awareness Community Health	←--- Spring Weather - Drug Prog. Helpers HLAY Curriculum-	Topics → Sizes - - Body Parts 2000, Units 1-7	←- Seeds → ←- Weights ----	Summer	Topics →
Skill/Centers Activity Time/Art		--Blocks Listening ---- Chalk	House- keeping Station Boards-	- Computer Manipulatives Fine Motor	- Clay/Play - Puzzles VCR	Dough – - Art Media (related	Seasonal - Library - Videos) ----	Interest	Centers	→

FIGURE 1.2 Kindergarten Curriculum Map

Source: Jacobs (1997), p. 73 (Map A).

evaluation to determine if the curriculum aligns properly. The extent to which these elements are synchronized (or asynchronized) will provide a clear picture of what essential questions (Jacobs, 1997) will need to be articulated to guide the curriculum design or redesign.

Curriculum Alignment

Since the advent of high-stakes testing and the emphasis on national and state standards as a basis for judging school effectiveness, administrators and teachers have felt considerable pressure to align the school curriculum with the state and national assessments that most states have legislated. As a result, curriculum alignment has come into practice in many school districts, but especially those with low-performing schools on state and national assessments. In general, the curriculum context for this process is at the macro-level (school or school district) because the intention is to either match the curriculum to the test (back-loading) or to make the test fit the curriculum by designing the curriculum first (front-loading) (English & Steffy, 2001, pp. 57–58).

Although the concept of curriculum alignment is discussed in more depth in Chapter 6 in the context of selecting and writing learning outcomes, curriculum alignment also plays an important role in the initial analysis of the existing curriculum context. Along with the curriculum audit and curriculum mapping, analyzing the degree of alignment or misalignment between the curriculum that currently exists and the desired outcomes to be assessed is essential in determining whether the curriculum needs to be redesigned or if a new curriculum needs to be created. This macroanalysis will also be helpful in determining whether the problem is with the curriculum or with the assessment device(s). Unfortunately, in this day of standardized assessments created by testing services or publishing companies, the test usually determines the curriculum.

However, as English and Steffy (2001, p. 59) point out, "deep" alignment goes beyond just tinkering with the existing curriculum and classroom teaching to fit the test. To them, the test is the place to start, but the redesign should include a serious analysis and discussion of the overall effectiveness of the entire learning environment, pedagogical practice, and the match between learner needs and the curriculum being taught (English & Steffy, p. 59). In the English and Steffy curriculum alignment model, both front-loading and back-loading involve the design and delivery of the curriculum. The *front-loading* process concerns writing the curriculum first and then writing the appropriate assessment (design) and teaching the curriculum first, putting what is taught on paper and then writing the assessment (delivery). In the *back-loading* process, publicly released test items are obtained and then a curriculum is created from them (design), and those test items are included as part of classroom practice and embedded in the curriculum content and classroom context (delivery) (English & Steffy, 2001, p. 58).

Although test designers and critical theorists alike may view the back-loading process of curriculum alignment with considerable consternation, the fact is that administrators and teachers in many school districts will feel forced to follow the back-loading model to survive the realities of high-stakes testing and the punitive nature of how those test results are interpreted and used.

The use of one or more of these analytical tools—the curriculum audit, curriculum mapping, and curriculum alignment—will provide useful information to curriculum designers as they decide whether the curriculum needs to be redesigned or if an entirely new design is warranted. The data from any of these analytical tools will be critical in framing the essential questions about what students need to know, do, and believe and what teachers need to emphasize in selecting, organizing, and delivering curriculum content in the classroom context. The next section will explore how to articulate these essential questions and their role in curriculum design.

Essential Questions

As Heidi Hayes Jacobs notes, essential questions "are an exceptional tool for clearly and precisely communicating the pivotal points of the curriculum" (Jacobs, 1997, p. 25). Essential questions are derived primarily from the curriculum maps, but they can also reflect what was disclosed by the macroanalyses done through a curriculum audit and/or as a result of efforts to align the curriculum. Essential questions articulate to the students what they are expected to learn. They are not as formulaic and staid as are course, unit, and lesson objectives (Jacobs, 1997, p. 28). The essential questions, which tell students the key concepts, skills, attitudes, and values they will encounter, are presented in a format that indicates that students should be able to answer them through the learning experiences in the curriculum. Jacobs (1997, pp. 30–33) identifies eight key criteria for the essential questions:

1. Each child should be able to understand the essential questions.

2. The questions should be written in broad, organizational terms (that is, they should communicate the "big picture" to the students and act as an advance organizer).

3. The questions should reflect conceptual priorities (that is, key concepts contained on concept maps).

4. Each question should be distinct and substantial (that is, it should not be ambiguous or focus on nonessential information).

5. Questions should not be repetitious (that is, they should relate to each other and be interconnected as in a latticework, but not require students to answer the same question in different formats).

6. Questions should be realistic given the amount of time allocated to the unit or course.

7. There should be a logical sequence to a set of essential questions (that is, the questions should be purposeful and lead to the outcomes of the unit or course).

8. The questions should be posted in the classroom.

Jacobs (1997, pp. 65–67) cites several examples of essential questions that reflect different grade levels and content areas:

- How does flight impact human beings?
  What is the future of flight?
  (fourth grade, interdisciplinary unit of six weeks)

- What is intelligence?
  How has intelligence evolved?
  (eleventh grade, AP biology interdisciplinary unit of four weeks)

- What is snow?
  How does it affect me?
  (first grade, interdisciplinary unit of three weeks)

- How does the physical environment of Japan impact its people?
  What is the structure of Japanese society?
  (ninth grade, English, social studies, humanities unit of six weeks)

The essential questions help focus the curriculum designer's efforts on why students need to learn the content and how that content can be contextualized for the learner. Even when the curriculum is mandated and the textbooks are selected by statewide committees, the classroom teacher still has to provide a context for the content or the learning will be largely meaningless for the student. The curriculum maps and essential questions tell the teacher and students what is important, what are the priorities, and what is the balance among learner, societal, and content needs. By using such processes as the curriculum audit, curriculum alignment, and curriculum mapping, the designer will be able to articulate clearly the essential elements of the curriculum and why they are important.

The following activities will help the designer establish these curricular priorities and provide the foundation for the design model and the purpose for the curriculum design or redesign. Although it will not be possible to do a curriculum audit or to align the curriculum for a macroanalysis in these activities, it will be possible to do a calendar-based curriculum map for a microanalysis of the existing curriculum context.

ACTIVITY 1.1   Creating a Calendar-Based Curriculum Map

1. Using the example in Figure 1.2, develop a curriculum map for the course or unit as it is currently being taught.
2. Working from that map, identify, add, and/or delete new topics, concepts, and skills that need to be considered in the new design or redesign.

Source: Jacobs (1997).

ACTIVITY 1.2   **Identifying Essential Questions to Establish Curricular Goals and Purpose**

Using the examples cited in the "Essential Questions" section, identify and enumerate a set of questions for the course or unit to be designed or redesigned. Be sure to use the eight criteria from Jacobs to screen the questions so that the questions will be useful for establishing the design's purpose.

Source: Jacobs (1997).

REFERENCES

Berns, R. G., & Erickson, P. M. (2001). Contextual teaching and learning: Preparing students for the new economy. The highlight zone: research @ work no. 5. Retrieved September 17, 2002, from http://nccte.com/publications/inforsynthesis/highlightzone/highlight05/highlight05-CTL.html

Cremin, L. (1964). *The transformation of the school* (pp. 135–142). New York: Vintage Books.

Dewey, J. (1902). *The child and the curriculum* (pp. 15–16). Chicago: University of Chicago Press.

Dewey, J. (1938). *Experience and education.* New York: Macmillan.

English, F. (1978). *Quality control in curriculum development* (pp. 26–31). Arlington, VA: American Association of School Administrators.

English, F. (2000). *Deciding what to teach and test: Developing, aligning, and auditing the curriculum* (pp. 64–119). Thousand Oaks, CA: Corwin Press.

English, F., & Steffy, B. (2001). *Deep curriculum alignment* (pp. 56–65). Lanham, MD: Scarecrow Press.

Howey, K. (1998). Introduction to the commissioned papers (pp. 19–33). In *Contextual teaching and learning.* Information Series No. 376. Columbus, OH: ERIC Clearinghouse on Adult, Career and Vocational Education and Washington, DC: ERIC Clearinghouse on Teaching and Teacher Education (co-publishers).

Jacobs, H. H. (1997). *Mapping the big picture: Integrating curriculum and assessment K–12* (pp. 1–16, 25–33, 73). Alexandria, VA: Association for Supervision and Curriculum Development.

Katz, M. (1973). The "new departure" in Quincy, 1873–81: The nature of nineteenth century educational reform. In M. Katz (Ed.), *Education in American history* (pp. 68–84). New York: Praeger Publishers.

Mondale, S. & Patton, S. (2001). *School: The story of American public education* (pp. 76–77, 86–91, 117–118). Boston: Beacon Press.

RECOMMENDED READINGS

Belenky, M. F., Clinchy, B. M., Goldberger, N. R., & Tarule, J. M. (1990). Connected teaching. In C. Conrad & J. Haworth (Eds.), *Curriculum in transition* (pp. 309–321). Needham, MA: Ginn Press (ASHE Reader Series).

Chiarelott, L. (December, 1978). John Dewey's theory of experience as a base for developing citizenship education curricula. *Educational Technology,* pp. 18–24.

Chiarelott, L. (Fall, 1983). The role of experience in the curriculum: Application of Dewey's theory of experience. *Journal of Curriculum Theorizing, 5*(4), 22–37.

Dewey, J. (1963). *The school and society* (p. 72). Chicago: University of Chicago Press.

Dewey, J. (1968). *Democracy and education* (p. 150). New York: Macmillan.

Pollock, R. (1960). Process and experience. In J. Blewett (Ed.), *John Dewey: His thought and influence* (pp. 174–191). New York: Fordham University Press.

Ratner, J. (1939). The pattern of reflective thinking. In J. Ratner (Ed.), *John Dewey's philosophy* (p. 851). New York: Random House.

2

Moving from Essential Questions to Statement of Purpose

The curriculum audit, curriculum maps, and curriculum alignment are useful tools for helping the curriculum designer generate the Essential Questions that learners should be able to answer after completing the curriculum. However, those questions need to be contextualized within the schema of the learners so that the learning outcomes, experiences, and activities are meaningful for the learners. This need requires the designer to provide a Statement of Purpose that clearly articulates *why* the curriculum is important and necessary for the learner to learn. The Statement of Purpose also reflects how the designer perceives the learner, society, and knowledge (content) needs and the balance among those needs in the curriculum design. This chapter will explore how various orientations to curriculum (Eisner & Vallance, 1974) can help designers see how they perceive learner, societal, and knowledge (content) needs and how those orientations can help designers understand exactly what the Statement of Purpose is communicating. Sample Statements of Purpose for each orientation will illustrate how the orientations are put into operation.

By definition, CTL curriculum designs place content/knowledge needs within the context of learner and societal needs. In this regard, content is made meaningful through its usefulness for and relevance to addressing both the individual needs of the learner and the problems faced by society either locally, nationally, or globally. This perspective on how content/knowledge, learner, and societal needs are expressed through the curriculum balances the three sources of curriculum upon the context within which learning is to occur. In other words, the context will largely determine which source will be emphasized and how the needs from each of the sources will be expressed in the curriculum design's Statement of Purpose discussed later in this chapter.

For example, in a problem-based curriculum, societal needs would most likely be the dominant source for determining the content of the curriculum, but it would also be important to assess the degree to which learners perceive those problems as relevant and useful to their lives. Conversely, a project-based curriculum would tend to emphasize an assessment of which of the learners' needs were being met through their individually designed projects, but those projects would also need to be placed within the context of larger societal issues and concerns.

These examples point up the dilemma that faces anyone who tries to write a curriculum design. Curriculum does not exist in a vacuum; it is shaped by needs while simultaneously meeting them. The product of the design process represents the manifestation of differing perspectives on needs and thus embodies the designer's beliefs about how needs are met most effectively. But where do these varying perspectives come from and how do they affect the structure and content of the curriculum design? The next section will examine how different orientations to curriculum view the needs of society, learners, and content.

In preparing to write a Statement of Purpose for a curriculum design, the sources of needs (learner, society, content) will be balanced according to which source the design will emphasize. Although all three sources will be addressed, it is unlikely that the final product will reflect an equal proportion of each source of needs. Most curriculum designs are content-based or combine content and societal needs. To a lesser extent, "pure" societal needs-based curriculum designs may also be emphasized, especially in problem-based models. Curriculum designs based solely on learner needs are rarest and would probably be most evident in a special-needs classroom.

The context for which the curriculum is being designed will largely dictate the balance reflected in the Statement of Purpose. However, most statements clearly reflect one or two orientations to curriculum, and these orientations tend to represent well-defined emphases on content, learner, and societal needs. After reviewing the orientations and analyzing the sample Statement of Purpose for each orientation, it will be essential to develop a statement and analyze it with a group of classmates or colleagues. Note that during the analysis of the examples for each orientation, not everyone will agree with the need(s) articulated in the sample statements, and this should be expected. The discussion of these samples should focus on the statement's consistency with the orientation it represents and then on how it might be changed to represent that orientation more effectively.

ORIENTATIONS TO CURRICULUM

Although most curriculum texts present an overview of philosophies of education (for example, humanistic, naturalistic, pragmatic) or curricular philosophies (essentialism, perennialism, experimentalism), Elliot Eisner and Elizabeth Vallance articulated a set of curriculum orientations that appear to be highly applicable to the design of CTL curriculum. First presented in their book *Conflicting Conceptions of Curriculum* (1974), the orientations were further developed by Eisner in his book *The Educational Imagination* (1979). Eisner and Vallance presented five different orientations: (a) academic rationalism; (b) development of cognitive processes; (c) personal relevance; (d) social adaptation/reconstruction; and (e) curriculum as technology. Of the five, only curriculum as technology appears to lack applicability to CTL curriculum design primarily because technology itself is a context. The other four orientations, however, do present multiple perspectives on teaching and learning and the roles societal, learner, and content/knowledge needs play in creating context.

Academic Rationalism

Of these four curriculum orientations, academic rationalism is perhaps the most decontextualized in its view of learner, societal, and content needs. Rooted in the classical modernist philosophy, academic rationalism supports an essentialist/perennialist view of education. Content/knowledge needs clearly predominate over learner and societal needs, although the academic rationalist would argue that learners who are well-versed in their cultural heritage can solve important individual and societal problems. In essence, a classically educated citizen is a "good" citizen.

With regard to content, the acquisition and storage of information and ideas is paramount. The well-educated person has a thorough grasp of the concepts and skills that comprise his or her cultural heritage. Familiarity with great works of literature, basic communication and computational skills (for example, the three Rs), foreign language(s), physical and life sciences, and the history of Western civilization are essential to a liberally educated person in the United States. The learner's mind is likened to a muscle that needs to be exercised and only certain types of rigorous content can train the mind effectively. Rather than acting on the content, the learner absorbs it, like a sponge. Testing should assess how much content the learner has absorbed and retained.

An educated populace can solve society's problems. Academic rationalists such as Hyman Rickover and Arthur Bestor believe that the curriculum should provide basic learning experiences for the general population of students and challenge intellectually the "best and brightest," who will become the leaders of the next generation. The school's curriculum should produce the corporate, political, scientific, and educational intelligentsia of the future while also enabling all who complete the curriculum to function successfully as members of the workforce and as citizens willing to participate actively to solve society's problems.

Because the content is not directly related to the context for academic rationalists, they believe that the educated person will be wise enough to apply his or her basic, liberal education to whatever context in which he or she functions. This concept of "massive general transfer" assumes that the educated person can transfer skills and knowledge without specific contextual preparation yet recognize when a particular skill or bit of knowledge fits across numerous contexts.

In the following sample Statement of Purpose, the writer presents a series of arguments about why seventh-grade students need a basic U.S. geography course.

Read through this example, try to identify where it addresses learner, content, and societal needs, and then analyze the evidence presented to determine why this writer believes that U.S. geography, in and of itself, is an important course for seventh graders. If this statement were critiqued in a small group, what revisions would group members recommend to the writer to make the statement more persuasive and convincing? In this example, as in this chapter's other examples, there may not be total agreement with the choice of orientation or the supporting arguments, but the intention is to identify the statement's consistency with the orientation and how it addresses and balances the three curricular sources (learner, society, content).

Sample Statement of Purpose

U.S. GEOGRAPHY, A ONE-SEMESTER COURSE FOR SEVENTH GRADERS. Geography is more than the study of the Earth. It is the study of how the environment enhances or limits our survival. It encourages an understanding of the human framework that has been established to overcome environmental limitations by utilizing necessary resources. This course is designed to introduce seventh-grade students to basic geographic concepts and the relationships that stem from those concepts. Using this information, students will be able to incorporate basic social studies ideas into their relationships with the world with greater success. All students need to have the basic information presented in this course to appreciate how people live and interact in the twenty-first century.

U.S. geography is intended to help students at this level come to an understanding of their physical position on Earth in relation to the total environment included within the boundaries of the United States. This understanding will increase the students' awareness of their city, county, state, and regional area and how it compares, contrasts, and relates to other regions in the U.S.A. This course will focus on using maps to identify location and direction and to explain regional population centers and reasons for their existence to assist in this understanding process. Further, the students will gain a better understanding of how geography affects city, state, regional, and national economies and, more importantly, their individual lifestyles. "Home" will take on a new meaning. Students will come to appreciate their environment through the study of various pollution concerns and the conservation efforts that have been initiated to save resources. Their understanding of geography will allow students to be more comfortable in their environment and, therefore, potentially more productive citizens.

Development of Cognitive Processes

As with the academic rationalist orientation, the development of cognitive processes also emphasizes content. However, this orientation operates from the perspective that information should be processed, not just acquired, stored, and retrieved when needed. Thus, how a learner acquires information and the thinking skills required to use that information effectively are of primary importance. Rather than content being an end in itself, it is a means to an end. The purpose of the curriculum is to create lifelong learners who know how to learn.

In the development of cognitive processes orientation, students learn cognitive strategies that transcend specific content areas. They become skilled at using the scientific method, problem-solving and decision-making strategies, and critical thinking skills. The curriculum designer and/or classroom teacher determines the content and the context in which those methods, strategies, and thinking skills develop, but the intent is to provide a general set of cognitive processes that can be transferred to a wide variety of settings.

Societal and learner needs are met by creating citizens who have a functional foundation of information and ideas, but who also know where to find additional information and ideas when the need arises. People are adaptable to learning new concepts and skills because they have learned how to learn. Intelligence is viewed as the ability to solve problems rather than the ability to recall specific information. Learners become more adept at constructing knowledge rather than acquiring and disseminating information.

This orientation depends heavily on the context in which learning occurs. It represents a functional, pragmatic approach to teaching and learning that focuses on *how* to learn rather than *what* to learn. The teacher becomes the "guide on the side" instead of the "sage on the stage," although the teacher still has considerable responsibility for determining both the content and the processes to be learned. Hence, the CTL curriculum design offers a significant degree of latitude to the teacher for selecting and sequencing the learning experiences that guide the development of cognitive processes.

The development of cognitive processes orientation stresses process over content, although content is embedded in the process. In the following sample Statement of Purpose, try to determine how this writer addresses process-oriented outcomes, concepts, and skills. How does this writer balance learner, societal, and content needs and does one of these needs appear to take precedence over the others? Try to identify the content base for the process being developed in this curriculum and, finally, the process being emphasized. Critique this statement in a small group and recommend revisions to the writer to make the statement more persuasive and convincing.

Sample Statement of Purpose

The ability to communicate needs, desires, ideas, and feelings is basic for survival. Our institutions—government, business, and especially schools—depend upon the efficient use of language. In schools, language becomes the vehicle or conduit for learning. We must be able to utilize language effectively to deal with the world in which we live.

Children acquire language through the primary skill of listening and they gradually learn to speak fluently. This occurs without formal instruction before they enter school. Assimilation of language by the child depends upon both inheritance and environment. Development of language patterns reflects to a great extent both home and community in which children live.

Once the child enters school, formal reading instruction begins, followed closely by instruction in writing. These two communication skills become the measure of literacy for the child. Reading brings recorded knowledge to the child in both prose and poetry form. Through reading, interests expand, attitudes change, and values are clarified. Writing permits an expression of creativity inherent in all children.

Children must be active participants in all phases of the language arts for a rich and varied language environment helps develop competence. Experience needs language to give it form. Language needs experience to give it content. The communication skills are taught most effectively in an instructional setting by integrating listening, speaking, reading, and writing. Language is an integral part of the way we present ourselves to others. Through language our appreciation of others deepens, and we are better able to manage the world in which we live. A full development of language is directly related to improvement of the quality of life.

Personal Relevance

In the personal relevance orientation, the learner's needs tend to dominate over societal or knowledge/content needs. This orientation posits that the learner is in the best position to assess his or her needs and what content meets those needs. The learner is perceived as someone who can make choices and take responsibility for them. The curriculum should be designed to provide those opportunities or to create an environment where making choices is the focus and students learn to take responsibility for those choices.

The learner acquires content and develops thinking processes whenever he or she decides that content or process is needed. The learner also determines the amount of time necessary to acquire that content or process and may spend considerably more time than another student does on one topic and considerably less time on another. Self-evaluation, peer evaluation, and/or teacher evaluation can assess the extent to which the learner has met the outcomes he or she selected.

Societal needs are met by creating citizens who can make choices and take responsibility for their actions. Because students will constantly derive personal meaning from learning experiences, they will also construct knowledge continuously. The construction of knowledge will also be a socially negotiated process as learners match up with and contend against the constructions of other students. Advocates of the personal relevance orientation argue that students who constantly struggle to make meaning from their experiences, construct knowledge from the meanings they've created, and then socially negotiate their personal meanings and knowledge with others will inevitably become informed, active citizens. More importantly, they will acquire both the information and the skills necessary to become critical thinkers.

In a CTL curriculum, the personal relevance orientation emerges from the projects that each student selects, designs, and evaluates. The project-based approach enables learners to set their own objectives, direct the learning experiences needed to meet those objectives, and evaluate when those objectives have been met successfully. The learner both determines and acts within the context(s) necessary to complete the project. Thus, for example, a learner concerned about the abysmal turnout of voters in a precinct surrounding the school may design a project to increase voter turnout for the next election by providing information, writing letters, and offering transportation and would be evaluated based on the results of these efforts.

The next example of a Statement of Purpose presents an interesting quandary because it appears to address a significant need that most learners would find personally relevant. However, the final orientation to be discussed, social adaptation, could also serve as the belief system that supports this curriculum. A unit on "bullying" can use either orientation for philosophic support because it represents a problem that is both personally meaningful and socially important, especially given the current national emphasis on this issue. Read through this Statement of Purpose, identify how and why it fits the personal relevance orientation and how student-directed projects could be the focal point for this curriculum. Then, after reading the section on the social adaptation orientation, try to determine how a unit on "bullying" could also use a problem-based learning approach to address the needs cited in the statement. Following that analysis, critique the statement from the perspective of both orientations and suggest how to make the arguments and evidence presented more persuasive and convincing either as a project-based or a problem-based curriculum.

Sample Statement of Purpose

According to the American School Counselor Association, one in four children is bullied and one in five children engages in bullying behavior, while the National Schools Safety Center estimates that 2.7 million children are victims of bullying every year. A few researchers, however, have found that up to 80 percent of children are bullied during their school careers (Maine Project Against Bullying, 2000). Whether it is physical, verbal, or emotional abuse, bullying is aggressive behavior that is deliberate, repetitive, and hurtful.

Violence is increasing in our schools and in society as a whole. Bullying behavior is one predictor of future aggression, and studies have shown that there is a strong correlation between bullying and criminal activity. The National Education Association, for example, estimates that one in four bullies in school will have a criminal record by age 30. Because aggressive behavior is learned early and becomes resistant to change, a bullying unit at the elementary level is imperative. By teaching students how to prevent and respond to bullying, they will not only be able to reduce its occurrence at school but also take that knowledge and skill into their homes and communities, contributing to a safer society.

Because bullying affects everyone—victims, bullies, and bystanders—an understanding of and skills to prevent and respond to it are important for students to possess. Victims, for example, often experience physical, emotional, and behavioral problems and may also be at risk for committing suicide or engaging in violent acts themselves. Victims may also be unable to concentrate in school because their attention is drawn away from learning, resulting in a drop in academic performance. As fear increases, so do absences, truancy, and dropout rates. In fact, the National Education Association estimates that 160,000 students miss school every day because of bullying. Along with victims, however, bystanders also suffer as a result of bullying. The school climate, for example, can become negative and frightening, interfering with student learning and achievement. Bystanders may feel fearful and unsafe in school while others may learn that bullying is acceptable behavior and, at some point, even begin to engage in it themselves.

A bullying unit must be implemented so that students have the opportunity to grow, learn, and develop to their full potential. As a result of this unit, students will learn the concepts, skills, and strategies that will help them effectively respond to and prevent bullying, creating a safe and welcoming school environment for all students.

Societal Adaptation/Reconstruction

The social adaptation/reconstruction orientation appears to emphasize societal needs most notably although from different directions. Social adaptation suggests that curriculum should provide experiences that enable learners to fit into society successfully. Students should acquire the concepts and skills necessary to succeed in a competitive world. Employers expect graduates to have mastered basic skills, developed a strong work ethic, and demonstrated responsible and dependable behavior throughout their school career. In recent years, more employers are expecting graduates to have both knowledge and skill with existing technology and the ability to adapt to new technology. In essence, an effective citizen contributes to the economic and social well-being of our society.

Social reconstruction, while also addressing societal needs, stresses the importance of the learner as a change agent. Given the current state of society, the only constant is change. Graduates must be capable of recognizing the need for and direction of change and, if necessary, force change to happen. A society doesn't survive unless it is constantly reconstructed according to this perspective. Adaptation also involves change both within oneself and within the environment. Social problems such as pollution, poverty, war, and social injustice involve fundamental changes individually and collectively both in attitudes and behavior. The social adaptation/reconstruction orientation argues that the content and the learners' needs must be met through recognizing and solving the dominant societal problems surrounding us.

The CTL curriculum strongly supports the problem-based approaches to teaching and learning that this orientation advocates. Social problems provide compelling contexts from which to draw learning experiences within the curriculum. The content becomes a dynamic, organic entity constantly changing, expanding, and emerging as problems are identified, analyzed, and resolved. Problems can either be identified and contextualized by the designer and/or classroom teacher or be negotiated with the learners as contexts emerge. So, the curriculum designer may identify terrorism as a social problem and determine appropriate content-based topics in literature, cultural studies, the arts, science, and mathematics that relate to the study of terrorism and have the students create problem-based projects that draw from various content areas.

The final Statement of Purpose example represents a social reconstruction orientation because it seeks to change the way evolution is taught by integrating it within the context of cross-cultural religious beliefs. Many public schools would probably reject this controversial approach. However, a truly social reconstructionist curriculum does challenge the status quo both in society and in the classroom. It crosses content boundaries because social problems cross content boundaries. Finally, rather than trying to avoid or reduce the conflict between science and religion on the topic of evolution, it addresses it head-on because the intention is to change societal views, not to adapt to them.

Analyze this Statement of Purpose; identify how this writer balances the needs of society, the learner, and content and how effectively supporting evidence develops the argument about why this course is needed. Finally, critique this statement in a small group, and make recommendations so that the statement is more persuasive and convincing.

Sample Statement of Purpose

One of the questions that high school students ask is, "Where did I come from?" Along with this question follow others, such as "How did we get here?" and "How do I relate to this world?" Adolescence is a time of questioning; young adults are curious about the world around them and how they interact with this world.

Currently, there is a debate about what should be taught in school: evolution or creationism. In December of 2002, the Ohio Department of Education adopted new Science Standards that state that evolution is to be taught in the science classroom. The controversy is that the religious community feels that the findings of the evolutionary theory prove that there is no God. This is untrue. In order to fully educate the youth of America, they should be presented with all the options that are available. From this knowledge comes the power to make their own decisions about the origin of life.

The purpose of this course is to educate students with all theories on the origin of life. This would include presenting many religious theories (for example, Christianity, Islam, Hinduism, Buddhism, Confucianism, Judaism, Animism, and Shinto) and science theories. Providing more than two viewpoints will allow students to become aware of other people's beliefs and cultural practices. It is important to have an understanding since many civil wars being fought in other countries are dealing with religious beliefs. The relevance of understanding other people's cultures is very important in our fast-paced world. We live in a very eclectic society with many multicultural microcommunities. Understanding other people's beliefs and cultures will only improve these encounters.

CTL AND THE CURRICULUM
ORIENTATIONS

Each of the four curriculum orientations can contribute to the design of CTL curriculum. From academic rationalism, the designer can draw essential concepts and skills that transcend time and space and are present in any contextual learning experience. The development of cognitive processes is driven by the contexts in which the thinking processes develop. Processes are never content or context–free and must be created through the active involvement with authentic situations. Each person will see different meanings from each context, and the projects people create will reflect what they perceive to be personally relevant and meaningful to them. No one perceives a book, a film, a speaker, or a museum exhibit in exactly the same way. How people fit into or change the social milieu is deeply affected by the context and their perception of whether adaptation or change is necessary. Problem solving is contextual, and individuals socially negotiate the processes by which they solve those problems.

ACTIVITY 2.1 **Writing a Statement of Purpose for Your CTL Curriculum**

1. Write a one- to two-page statement that clearly indicates to the reader why the proposed curriculum needs to be designed or re-designed.
2. Include in the statement how your design addresses content/knowledge, societal, and learner needs. Provide supporting evidence from research or educational literature

that indicates why these needs are essential to your curriculum (for example, national/state standards, developmental theory and research, social theory and research).
3. After you create your draft statement, analyze it based upon each of the orientations to see which one(s) you've emphasized.

Although each of these orientations has some applicability to the design of curriculum in general and CTL curriculum specifically, the dilemma the designer faces is how these orientations will affect the actual design. In reviewing each of these orientations, most educators find themselves either within or across one or more of the orientations. It would be unusual to find someone who could not locate himself somewhere in the orientations. In fact, it might be more likely to find someone who saw some of her educational philosophy in each of the orientations depending on, as might be expected, the *context*.

Because context usually drives educational philosophies, the designer must decide how to use the orientations to construct the Statement of Purpose, or rationale, that will explain to the person using the curriculum why and how the designer balanced content/knowledge, societal, and learner needs and how the final design reflects that balance. Activity 2.1 requires writing a Statement of Purpose for a CTL curriculum and explaining how and why it reflects any or all of the orientations discussed and how it balances content/knowledge, societal, and learner needs.

REFERENCES

Eisner, E. (1979). *The educational imagination* (pp. 61–86). New York: Macmillan.

Eisner, E., & Vallance, E. (Eds.). (1974). *Conflicting conceptions of curriculum*. Berkeley, CA: McCutchan.

3

∾

Overview of Curriculum Design Process and Models

The use of analytical tools and procedures such as the curriculum audit, curriculum mapping, and curriculum alignment provides the data for determining the essential questions to help identify major focal points of the curriculum design. These questions then serve as the springboard for establishing the purpose for curriculum change, which would be contextualized within and/or among various curriculum orientations. Now that a purpose for curriculum change has been established and contextualized across the needs of society, the learner, and knowledge (content), it is time to begin the actual curriculum design through a model that is applicable to macro-design needs (for example, programmatic, grade level, district-level changes) and micro-design needs (courses, unit-level changes).

The model for designing CTL curricula is derived from and influenced by a classical, historical framework, the Tyler rationale (Tyler, 1949), and a contemporary model, the Wiggins and McTighe backward design (Wiggins & McTighe, 1998, pp. 7–19). By combining a classical and contemporary model, the design model used in this text draws from Tyler's four key design questions, which have informed and guided virtually every curriculum design since 1949 but which also have been heavily criticized because of their linearity. To balance this criticism, the Wiggins and McTighe model is used to stress to the designer that curriculum design rarely unfolds in as neat a linear sequence as Tyler's model suggests. Rather, it is a dynamic, free-flowing, interactive process that can unfold in a backward direction as well.

An examination of the Tyler rationale and the Wiggins and McTighe backward design will illustrate the key components of each model. This examination will help orient designers to the CTL curriculum design model that this text uses.

THE TYLER RATIONALE

Since 1949, the work of Ralph Tyler has dominated the procedural perspective in American curriculum design. Using his syllabus from a curriculum course he was teaching at the University of Chicago as the basis for his book, Tyler published *Basic Principles of Curriculum and Instruction* (Tyler, 1949). Although Tyler drew heavily from the scientific management curriculum theorists of the 1920s, such as W. W. Charters, Franklin Bobbitt, and David Snedden (Eisner, 1985), his reputation as the head of the evaluation team for the Eight-Year Study clearly helped establish his book as the pre-eminent design text of the latter half of the twentieth century.

Tyler's Four Questions

The Tyler rationale essentially consists of four questions Tyler posed as he sought to structure the curriculum design process. These questions aimed to guide curriculum designers as they sought to identify and connect the component parts of the curriculum:

- What educational purposes should the school seek to attain?
- How can learning experiences be selected that are likely to be useful in attaining these objectives?
- How can learning experiences be organized for effective instruction?
- How can the effectiveness of learning experiences be evaluated?

By locating the purposes/outcomes question first and the evaluation question last in his text, one could infer that the design process begins with the delineation of educational objectives and ends with the evaluation of whether curriculum objectives have been met. However, a closer examination of Tyler's evaluation approach indicates that outcomes play an important role in evaluation, implying that one could start and end the process with evaluation. Even with this generous interpretation of Tyler's four questions and the order in which one addresses them, however, the argument that procedural models are linear in structure is valid.

The graphic depiction of the Tyler rationale (see Figure 3.1) clearly suggests a linearity that has been widely criticized since the early 1970s (Kliebard, 1975). However, while the rational linearity of the steps in Tyler's model may be open to justified critique, the four questions he posed as the basis for the Tyler rationale still warrant serious consideration from a procedural perspective. The issue of where one starts and ends the process will always be open to debate, especially when designing a contextual curriculum, but the questions themselves frame the

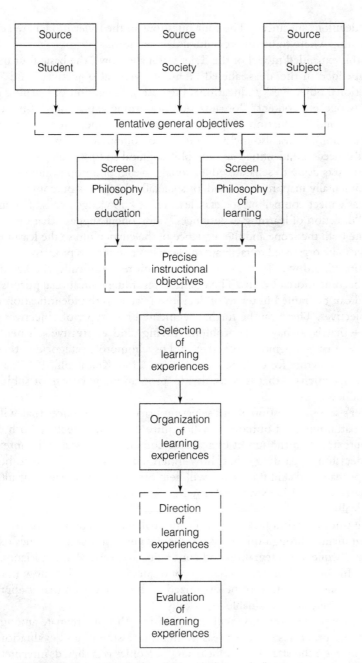

FIGURE 3.1 Tyler's Curriculum Rationale (expanded)

Source: From P. F. Oliva, *Developing the Curriculum,* 3rd ed., 1992, p. 169. Reprinted by permission of HarperCollins Publishers.

design decisions succinctly. The four questions in the Tyler model are central to determining where to begin procedural deliberations.

As this expanded model of the Tyler rationale shows, the basic four questions are embedded in the areas labeled "tentative general objectives" and "precise instructional objectives" (educational purposes), "selection of learning experiences" (scope and content), "organization of learning experiences" (structure and sequence), and "evaluation of learning experiences" (measurement, assessment, and evaluation). Oliva also includes a depiction of curricular sources from which curricular needs are identified and the philosophical and psychological screens that Tyler suggests using to separate educationally weak, philosophically inconsistent, developmentally inappropriate, and/or societally dangerous outcomes from those that clearly meet compelling societal, learner, or knowledge needs. The inclusion of the "direction of learning experiences" component suggests that one needs to articulate both the scope and the sequence of the curriculum so the learning experiences can be organized to facilitate the learner's continuous progress.

In breaking down Tyler's four questions more specifically, the key decision points become more obvious. The question regarding educational purposes to be attained can be framed in terms of decisions related to the identification of goals and objectives. These can be further segmented into types of objectives or outcomes—that is, behavioral, problem solving, and expressive (Eisner, 1985); domains—that is, cognitive, affective, and psychomotor; categories—that is, the taxonomic structure for each domain (Bloom, 1956; Krathwohl, 1964); and even levels of specificity—that is, schoolwide, programmatic course or subject area, unit, and lesson plans.

Tyler's second question about selecting learning experiences that will facilitate the attainment of outcomes will require decisions affecting both content and context. Given the surfeit of available content, processes, and contexts, difficult decisions regarding what, how much, and when will need to be made. Concept maps and skill flowcharts will help organize the choices, but ultimately the question of "What's worth knowing?" will force options to be narrowed dramatically.

The third question poses a significant challenge to curriculum articulation and alignment. Through this question, the designer must address issues related to scope and sequence, integration and continuity, and vertical and horizontal articulation. In conjunction with Tyler's second question, the what, how much, and when responses will need to be organized within a structure that is appropriate developmentally and sustainable logistically.

Tyler's evaluation question will force decisions that differentiate among related but distinct processes such as measurement, assessment, and evaluation. How information on the attainment of learning outcomes is gathered, interpreted, and judged is crucial to this phase of the design. In addition, it will be necessary to decide how to use the information collected to change the curriculum design both formatively and summatively. Finally, it will be important to convey how the evaluation flows through the design that's been created and is an ongoing rather than a terminal phase in the curriculum.

THE WIGGINS AND MCTIGHE
BACKWARD DESIGN

In 1998, Grant Wiggins and Jay McTighe created a curriculum design model using what they termed a "backward design" approach (Wiggins & McTighe, 1998, pp. 7–19). This model has received considerable attention, largely because it appears to capture the essential elements in Tyler's four questions but in three distinct stages. It identifies three major components of curriculum design (outcomes, assessment, and learning experiences) while also keeping the designer focused on the connection between learning and instruction. This is particularly relevant to curriculum design in early childhood settings where greater emphasis is usually placed on children's learning and development rather than content-specific standards and outcomes. Although the Wiggins and McTighe model has applicability across a variety of learning environments, it may be best used in a learner-centered design rather than a subject-centered or society-centered design. As later chapters demonstrate, the appropriate design model is directly related to the curricular source (learner, society, content/knowledge) emphasized in the final product of the design.

In Figure 3.2, the three stages of Wiggins and McTighe model are clearly delineated. This model suggests that teachers begin with the end (results or standards) and thus create a backward design (Wiggins & McTighe, p. 8). Essentially, Tyler also suggested this in his four questions, and Wiggins and McTighe acknowledge this (p. 8). However, they also point out that teachers usually begin thinking about design by focusing first on the content and learning activities rather than the outcomes. This echoes the findings of John Zahorik (1975), who found a similar phenomenon in his research (see Chapter 6 for more detail on this research).

Wiggins and McTighe also note that assessment should be considered early in the design process (pp. 8–9), a departure from other models and, to some extent, from Tyler's four questions, which focused on assessment and evaluation as the final design step. Thus, the notion of a "backward design" is partially correct in that it does mirror a departure from reality with regard to the way teachers typically plan. However, in fairness, other design models do emphasize desired outcomes first, although they tend not to emphasize assessment as early as Wiggins and McTighe do. In that regard, particularly, the Wiggins and McTighe model represents an important departure from, and contribution to, the literature on curriculum design models.

The structure of the Tyler rationale underscores the importance of his four questions that guide the curriculum designer in setting appropriate objectives, selecting learning experiences, organizing those experiences, and evaluating the effectiveness of the design in helping the learner attain the objectives. However, the Wiggins and McTighe backward design highlights the need for the designer to see the four questions in a dynamic, fluid relationship so that the design emerges from the context in which the designer is working.

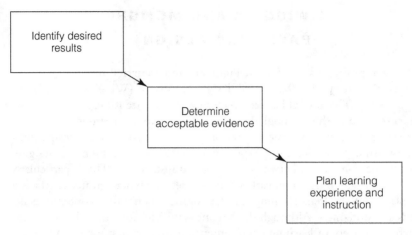

FIGURE 3.2 Wiggins and McTighe's "Backward Design"

Source: From Wiggins and McTighe, *Understanding by Design,* 1998, p. 9. Reprinted by permission of the Association for Supervision and Curriculum Development.

Standards-Based Curriculum Design

Many teachers are turning to standards-based approaches as a way to integrate both knowledge/content needs and social problem solving. Virtually all discipline-based learned societies—for example, the National Association for the Education of Young Children and the National Council of Teachers of Mathematics—have articulated a set of national standards that have been adopted by and then adapted to each state. In most cases, these standards provide a set of outcomes, albeit highly general, that teachers can use as the conceptual base for their curriculum designs.

Statewide proficiency tests and other state and national high-stakes, normative assessments are forcing local school districts, and consequently classroom teachers, to incorporate national and state standards into their courses of study. As a result, knowledge of these standards becomes an essential element of the design process for teachers.

In a sense, then, standards create a societal context for creating curriculum locally. They are a social force over which teachers have little control but to which they must respond. By using the standards as the conceptual base for their curriculum designs, teachers should be able to identify key concepts, skills, attitudes, and values that provide the foundational content for the curriculum. By placing these concepts, skills, attitudes, and values into the context of social problem solving, teachers can integrate outcomes that form the basis for normative assessments into meaningful learning experiences that address critical social problems.

The national standards are too lengthy to include in this text, and most states have their own versions of standards for each content area. You can access national standards at the websites in Appendix C. After reaching the national website, access the individual state standards through the links provided. In addition, each State Department of Education allows access to individual state standards directly.

In either case, the sites furnish a substantial resource for building a standards-based curriculum.

In Chapter 4, the design model used in *Curriculum in Context* is described in terms of its major components, but it is presented as a product rather than a process. The product contains five components, and although each component is created separately, they are inextricably intertwined with each other. For that reason, each component is in a state of flux until the "final" product is finished. Chapter 4 will provide an overview of each component and will describe sequencing and evaluating the curriculum in more detail than the components of concept mapping, writing appropriate outcomes, organizing the curriculum into units or subunits, and writing a statement of purpose. Because the latter components require a deeper analysis due to their greater complexity and the wealth of misconceptions surrounding them, they will be discussed in separate chapters.

For example, the Statement of Purpose has already been discussed in the context of curriculum orientations in Chapter 2. Concept mapping will be discussed in Chapter 5 in the context of concept learning and the construction of knowledge. Chapter 6 will cover writing educational outcomes and organizing them within units in the context of aligning and balancing the curriculum. Finally, as a bridge to creating contextual instructional designs that Chapters 8, 9, and 10 will discuss, two of the most popular CTL models, problem/project-based learning (PBL) and service learning, will be explored in Chapter 7. In addition to establishing the use of PBL and service learning as both macro- and micro-design models, Chapter 7 will also establish them as critical models for instructional design in contextual teaching and learning environments.

The product design model in Chapter 4 may also be helpful as a basis for analyzing and explicating each component with smaller groups (four to six members) of educators. As each component is designed in draft form, it should be shared with other educators for feedback and critique. Consider each component as a work in progress. As each component is shared and critiqued, revise it based on the feedback and keep it under revision until the design is completed. Thus, Chapter 4 serves as the thematic connection across the curriculum design portion of this text. In that sense, Chapter 4 will provide the skeletal outline and Chapters 5 and 6 will provide the substance for the design of the contextual curriculum.

REFERENCES

Bloom, B. S. (1956). *Taxonomy of educational objectives: Cognitive domain.* New York: David McKay.

Doll, W. E. (1993). *A post-modern perspective on curriculum.* New York: Teachers College Press.

Eisner, E. W. (1985). The educational imagination: On the design and evaluation of school programs. New York: Macmillan.

Kliebard, H. (1975). Reappraisal: The Tyler rationale. In W. Pinar (Ed.), *Curriculum theorizing* (pp. 70–83). Berkeley, CA: McCutchan.

Krathwohl, D. R. (Ed.). (1964). *Taxonomy of educational objectives: Affective domain.* New York: David McKay.

Oliva, P. F. (1992). *Developing the curriculum* (3rd ed.). New York: HarperCollins.

Posner, G. J., & Ruditsky, A. N. (2001). *Course design: A guide to curriculum development for teachers* (6th ed.). New York: Longman.

Saylor, J. G., & Alexander, W. M. (1974). *Curriculum planning: Bases and processes.* New York: Holt, Rinehart and Winston.

Tyler, R. W. (1949). *Basic principles of curriculum and instruction.* Chicago: University of Chicago Press.

Wiggins, G., & McTighe, J. (1998). *Understanding by design* (pp. 7–19). Alexandria, VA: ASCD (Association for Supervision and Curriculum Development) Publications.

Zahorik, J. (1972). Teachers' planning models. *Educational Leadership, 33*(2), 134–139.

4

Designing a Curriculum for Contextual Teaching and Learning

Previous chapters focused on the basic elements of contextual teaching and learning, essential questions that guide the curriculum design process, and various orientations to curriculum. Those discussions provided the foundation for the articulation of a statement of purpose, and will provide the framework for the concepts, skills, attitudes, and beliefs selected and then organized through concept maps.

We can now create a complete curriculum design by taking Ralph Tyler's four fundamental design questions and organizing the responses to those questions in a format that facilitates contextual teaching and learning. To review, Tyler's four questions are:

1. What educational purposes should we seek to attain?
2. How can learning experiences be selected that are likely to be useful in attaining these objectives?
3. How can those experiences be organized for effective instruction?
4. How can the effectiveness of learning experiences be evaluated?

Figure 4.1 represents these questions visually so the actual final design product has a concrete reference point. The final design should contain the following components:

1. A statement of purpose that clearly articulates why the curriculum design (or redesign) is necessary and how the design will meet the needs of the learner and society and for knowledge. The statement should be brief (one

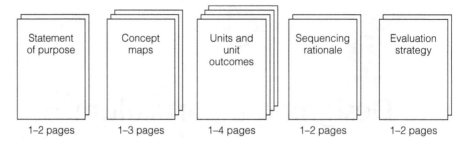

FIGURE 4.1 Format of a Sample Curriculum Design

to two pages) and provide compelling evidence that the curriculum has a solid conceptual, theoretical, and empirical base.

2. Create a concept map for each of the major areas identified based on major concepts, skills, attitudes, and beliefs referenced in the Statement of Purpose. In most cases, the maps will identify 20 to 30 concepts, themes, and/or topics and will fit on one 8½" × 11" page. Typically, one to three maps are sufficient. Depending on the focus of the curriculum, you may need more maps. These maps will be discussed more fully in Chapter 5 and through the examples in Appendix A.

3. From the major concepts, subconcepts, and coordinate concepts identified on the maps, break the curriculum down into units, subunits, subtopics, and so on. These organizational structures will provide the basis for identifying and listing unit, subunit, and lesson outcomes for the instructional design phase. The unit (or subunit) outcomes at this stage of the design will probably require three to six pages. State them so that you can accurately assess their attainment. Chapter 6 will present the different formats for these outcomes.

4. Once the units and unit outcomes have been selected and categorized, list the units (or subunits) in the order in which they will be taught. To explain the organizational scheme, include a one- or two-page sequencing rationale that describes the sequence selected, why it best fits the curriculum designed, and how the curriculum will follow that sequence.

5. The design structure will be evaluated from a formative and summative perspective, so you need to describe your evaluation strategy to ensure that the curriculum design components actually enable learners to meet the outcomes identified. Limit this description of the strategy to one to two pages. Both the sequencing rationale and the evaluation strategy will be discussed in this chapter.

When completed, the final product should be structured as shown in Figure 4.1.

The following sections will review the key points regarding the development of the statement of purpose and will describe how to select and categorize units and unit outcomes, sequence the units selected, and evaluate the final curriculum design.

DEVELOPING A MEANINGFUL
STATEMENT OF PURPOSE

Chapter 2 required writing a rough draft of a Statement of Purpose for the curriculum being designed. That statement should include descriptions of the learner, content, and societal needs that would be met through the curriculum. To determine if the Statement of Purpose provides compelling support for the design, have it analyzed and critiqued by a group of four or five colleagues or classmates.

The analysis and critique of the Statement of Purpose should address the following key points:

1. Does the Statement of Purpose briefly describe (one to two pages) the learner, content/knowledge, and societal needs that will be met through this curriculum? The learner needs should be age and developmentally appropriate and not simply transitory interests or wants. Societal needs may reflect a macro- (that is, global or national) or micro- (local or community) society orientation, but in either case, they should be contextual. Content/knowledge needs should stress the extent to which the concepts, skills, attitudes, and beliefs are relevant to the variety of contexts in which learners find themselves.

2. Does the Statement of Purpose suggest a particular orientation(s) to curriculum, and if so, how does that orientation reflect a balance of learner, societal, and content/knowledge needs? Note that balance indicates an appropriate proportion of each set of needs, not an equal amount. Indeed, depending on the focus of the curriculum design, one set of needs may be considerably more evident than the others. The result may suggest a more dominant/less dominant perspective on needs rather than an effort to cover each curricular source equally.

3. Does the Statement of Purpose communicate its message in a manner that a variety of audiences—for example, colleagues, community members, parents, and, if appropriate, students—can read and comprehend? As such, the statement should be relatively jargon free (for example, the term "constructivist" may not carry the same or any meaning across all audiences). When possible, either briefly define a specialized term or find a synonym that is more universally understood. Because the statement should also be convincing and persuasive, it may need to include references that provide empirical, philosophical, or conceptual support for assertions that might not be universally accepted. This evidentiary support can be very useful, especially with a controversial curriculum change (for example, whether to use evolution or intelligent design or both as the basis for high school biology curriculum). Try to use widely recognized research, national standards, and/or large-scale studies as references whenever possible.

4. Does your Statement of Purpose focus on the *curriculum* design (*what* will be taught) rather than the *instructional* design (*how* it will be taught)? Remember, the purpose is to convince the reader that the curriculum is worth learning. How the curriculum will be taught will be the focus of the instructional design.

5. Finally, is the Statement of Purpose convincing to others? Does it clearly describe "what" and "why" rather than simply list objectives for the learner to attain? Ultimately, the purpose is to persuade the reader that what is being taught is worth learning and that the design can make the learning relevant and meaningful to the learner. It answers the question "Why do I have to learn this?"

CREATING A CONCEPT MAP

Although creating a concept map or maps may be the most difficult task in the curriculum design process, it is also the most useful. The maps that will be developed in Chapter 5 should literally provide a "road map" to the major concepts, skills, attitudes, beliefs, themes, and/or topics in the curriculum. As colleagues/classmates analyze and critique the map(s), they should focus on the following areas:

1. Does the concept map depict clearly and accurately the superordinate, coordinate, and subordinate relationships between and among the major concepts on the map? Is it possible to explain these relationships verbally and the logic underlying the structure of the map?

2. Are the needs identified in the Statement of Purpose evident on the concept map? Are there clear connections among purpose and concepts, skills, processes, and other factors?

3. Does the concept map facilitate the identification of conjunctive, disjunctive, and relational concepts? Where are those concepts located in the map?

4. Finally, could the map serve as an assessment tool to determine if learners could actually locate and label the concepts accurately if given a blank copy of the map's structure? Practitioners who use concept maps in their teaching have suggested that an accurate method for determining if learners "see" the concepts they've learned contextually is to give them a blank map as a preassessment and a postassessment device. This would suggest that a correctly designed map can serve effectively as a curricular component, an instructional device, and an assessment tool.

IDENTIFYING UNITS AND WRITING
UNIT OUTCOMES

In many cases, the concept maps will serve as the best source for identifying the units (or subunits) for the curriculum design. The units may correspond directly with the major superordinate and coordinate concepts located in the most inclusive levels of the maps. However, you can combine two or more of these groupings into one unit title or group different areas of the concept map thematically or topically. Ultimately, the teaching units in the instructional design should be traceable to the concept map(s) created to depict the major concepts students need to attain.

The unit outcomes written for each unit (or subunit) will be stated at a level of specificity that can be assessed formally or informally through a variety of traditional and alternative assessment techniques. However, they will typically not be as detailed or specific as the daily lesson outcomes written for the instructional plans in the instructional design.

The actual form of the outcome statements may be behavioral, problem solving, or expressive (Eisner, 1979; 1985). Although the behavioral model dominated the format for writing objectives since the 1920s and had enjoyed a rebirth in the 1960s with the publication of Benjamin Bloom's *Handbook for Formative and Summative Evaluation* of Student Learning in 1971, and the subsequent work of Popham (1969), Mager (1962), and Gagné and Briggs (1979), Elliot Eisner (1969) proposed an expanded concept of educational outcomes in "Instructional and Expressive Objectives: Their Formulation and Use in Curriculum." In this article, he proposed three levels of objectives that he simply titled Type I, Type II, and Type III. In *The Educational Imagination* (1979), he named these levels behavioral (Type I), problem-solving (Type II), and expressive (Type III) outcomes.

These three types of outcomes differ from each other significantly both in form and substance. Behavioral objectives are stated in such a way that the learner knows both the problem to be solved and the manner in which the solution must be presented (Eisner, 1979). Typically, behavioral objectives have *one* correct solution—for example, a word is either spelled correctly or it isn't and a column of numbers is either added correctly or it isn't—and the singular solution is immediately measurable and/or observable. Well-stated behavioral objectives follow a well-defined abcd formula. It must have an *audience* (that is, the learner or student), a clear *behavior* (identify the reproductive parts of a flower), a set of *conditions* or *criteria* (a diagram of a flower), and the *degree* of mastery (90 percent accuracy). Thus, the well-stated behavioral objective would read: "Given a diagram of a flower, the student will be able to identify the reproductive parts of the flower with 90 percent accuracy." With this type of objective, the teacher can easily determine if a student can successfully perform this task using only one of a variety of measurement techniques.

As a cautionary note, however, writing a behavioral objective requires more than simply following an abcd formula. A well-written behavioral objective should focus on what students will *learn,* not just on what they will *do.* In addition, the statement should also make sense! For example, the statement "Given a map of the world, a student should be able to identify Mexico with 90 percent accuracy" seems to follow the abcd formula, and it also indicates a measurable skill that can be learned. However, it's a nonsensical statement because of the degree of mastery. Once the student has found Mexico on the map, he or she has found it. If a student requires nine incorrect guesses before locating Mexico, it's unlikely that much, if any, learning has occurred. Conversely, if the student locates Mexico on the first try, why have him or her repeat the behavior nine more times? In short, make sure the behavior is worth learning and measuring.

Problem-solving (Type II) objectives are written so that the problem is given but not the solution. This is because there are multiple (perhaps an infinite number) of potential correct solutions to the problem. These outcomes tend to be contextual in nature because they require learners to apply concepts to specific situations. For example, consider this problem: "Given a monthly spendable income of $2,000, the student will plan a budget for a family of four, including housing, food, clothing, entertainment, savings, and automobile payments." This type of outcome has no *one* correct response, although the teacher and learner can assess the successful attainment of the outcome by determining if the problem has been solved.

Problem-solving outcomes are designed for learning situations that tend to allow for multiple interpretations, perspectives, and solutions. They extend and expand upon outcomes achieved through behavioral objectives by applying the behaviors acquired to new or different situations. Thus, they are not antithetical to behavioral objectives but rather represent another point on the continuum of learning experiences. Obviously, they would be highly applicable to problem-based curricula.

Expressive (Type III) outcomes represent a significant departure from how educators are typically taught to write objectives. This is because neither the problem nor the solution is stated before the learning experience (Eisner, 1979; 1985). Instead, it offers a description of an "expressive encounter" (Eisner, 1979) that has the potential to provide a meaningful learning experience for the students. However, due to the nature of the expressive encounter, the learning outcome can't be stated until after the expressive encounter has occurred, and usually the learner, rather than the teacher, states the outcome. Because the learning outcome results from the expressive encounter, it does not predict the outcome as do behavioral and, to some extent, problem-solving objectives. Examples of expressive encounters include field trips, films, externships, internships, and student-generated projects. Thus, expressive outcomes represent yet another point on the continuum of learning experiences and would be particularly applicable to project-based or experientially based curricula.

Following the identification of unit outcomes, you may want to categorize them to determine if the balance among the outcomes fits the design of your curriculum. In addition to determining if the behavioral, problem-solving, and expressive outcomes are adequately balanced, also assess if the levels of cognition, affect, and skill are appropriate. There are many fine models for categorizing the cognitive domain, the affective domain, and the psychomotor domain (see Chapter 6 for a detailed description of some of these models). Select one model for each domain.

To summarize:

1. Select and group units based on the concept map(s) and/or make them easily traceable to the major areas of the map either thematically or topically.

2. Have 10 to 12 unit-level outcomes for each teaching unit, and use behavioral, problem-solving, and expressive outcomes when appropriate.

3. Classify each of the outcomes in the units according to a well-defined categorization scheme for each domain.

4. Ensure that the balance among types of outcomes and the levels in each domain are appropriate to the structure and substance of the curriculum design.

SELECTING A SEQUENCE
FOR THE CURRICULUM

Ralph Tyler's third question for guiding curriculum design asks, "How can learning experiences be organized for effective instruction?" We have already looked at issues related to the *scope* of the curriculum (mapping concepts, selecting units and unit outcomes), but organization also involves the *sequencing* of learning experiences. At this point, you must decide the order in which learning experiences will be presented to the learner. Because this is a *curriculum* sequence, there should only be *one* sequence for the entire design. This differs from the sequencing of instructional activities, which may involve the use of several sequencing patterns depending on the purpose and content of the lesson's activities. Although several sequencing patterns could fit the curriculum design, choose the one that works best for the teacher, the learners, and the content being taught. The sequencing rationale will explain (and perhaps defend) the reasons for the choice.

According to Posner and Strike (1976), there are five general categories of sequencing patterns with approximately 15 to 20 subcategories of more specific sequencing patterns. This categorization scheme is meant to be descriptive (describing possible choices) rather than prescriptive (prescribing the *one* best sequencing pattern to use when organizing the curriculum). In their text, *Course Design,* Posner and Rudnitsky (2001) have continued to refine the categorization scheme first described by Posner and Strike (1976). Figure 4.1 represents an adaptation and explanation of that categorization scheme.

Assess these sequencing patterns based upon a "best fit" model for the curriculum design. Although competing sequencing patterns make the process more complex, base your choice on such variables as the developmental level and age of the students, the structure of the content area being taught, the resources available, and ultimately the teachers' own beliefs about what constitutes a best fit. State the reasons behind the choice in a sequencing rationale by explaining first the selection of a sequencing pattern and then how that pattern will be put into operation through the organization of the units and subunits in the curriculum design.

I. World-related:

  A. Space—sequence based on naturally occurring physical location (for example, planets, physical geography, Earth's strata)

  B. Time—sequence based on chronological order (for example, literary periods, U.S. history, evolution)

  C. Physical attributes—sequence based on the order in which physical characteristics occur (for example, geological structures, anatomy and physiology, human development)

II. Concept-related:

  A. Class relations—sequence based on similar criteria within a category (for example, vertebrates, polygons, nouns and verbs)

(continued)

FIGURE 4.1 Sequencing Patterns

B. Propositional relations—sequence based on similar criteria within sets of propositions for example, Newton's Laws of Motion, atomic theory)

C. Sophistication—sequence based on level of complexity of the concepts being taught so that simpler concepts are taught before more complex concepts (for example, single-celled life forms are taught before multicelled life forms, elements before compounds)

D. Logical prerequisite—sequence based upon what appears to be logically antecedent and consequent (for example, addition, subtraction, multiplication, division, cause and effect)

III. Inquiry-related:

A. Logic of inquiry—sequence based on some logical structure for inquiry (for example, scientific method, critical thinking models)

B. Methods of inquiry—sequence based on how inquiry actually occurs within contexts (for example, methods used by physical scientists, social scientists, literary critics, film critics)

IV. Learning-related:

A. Empirical prerequisite—sequence based on what empirical research has suggested (for example, research on phonics-based sequences, Ausubel's verbal learning model)

B. Familiarity—sequence based on teaching what is most familiar to students first (most familiar to least familiar)

C. Difficulty—sequence based on level of difficulty for learners to learn the concept or skill (for example, least difficult skill or part of skill to most difficult)

D. Interest—sequence based on students' level of interest in the concept or skill (for example, most interesting topic to least interesting based on interest survey or inventory)

E. Development—sequence based on developmental model (for example, Vygotsky's zone of proximity, Piaget's stages of cognitive development)

F. Internalization—sequence based on the manner in which learners acquire a belief or attitude (for example, Krathwohl and Bloom's affective domain, Kohlberg's stages of moral development)

V. Utilization-related:

A. Procedure—sequence based on following a defined process in a particular context (for example, writing an essay, science laboratory procedures, car engine repair procedures)

B. Anticipated frequency of use—sequence based on how often a particular concept or skill will be used in a context (for example, job-related skills used daily versus those used rarely, software use versus. computer programming)

FIGURE 4.1 Sequencing Patterns (continued)

WRITING AN EVALUATION STRATEGY

Throughout the design process, your strategy for evaluating whether the curriculum design will actually result in the intended learning outcomes needs to be conceptualized. Assessing student learning is only one part of the data to be considered as the curriculum design is evaluated. Other data sources might include teachers, parents, and administrators and involve a variety of techniques for gathering and interpreting data. The strategy created will have a *formative* and a *summative* component to determine if the curriculum design is as strong as it possibly can be. Before I describe how to incorporate a formative and summative component, let's differentiate among the terms *measurement, assessment,* and *evaluation* because they are frequently used, erroneously, as synonymous concepts.

MEASUREMENT, ASSESSMENT, AND EVALUATION

Curriculum evaluation involves using various techniques for gathering and interpreting information and then making a judgment based on the interpretation of the information. We use *measurement* devices to gather information, and they are generally "objective" sources of data such as test scores, surveys, attendance records, weight, and height. We use *assessment* techniques to help interpret the data gathered through measurement. Observations, interviews, and portfolios of work completed can all extend the results of the measurement phase, but the intention is to give meaning to the numbers and/or to put a "face on the statistics." After gathering and interpreting data, the designer must make a judgment based on accepted external and/or internal criteria to effectively *evaluate* the design process. The stronger the data and the more meaningful the interpretation, the more defensible the evaluation.

This is analogous to the trial process in the legal system: evidence is collected using scientific data gathering techniques (measurement), the lawyers interpret the data for the judge and/or jury using multiple perspectives (assessment), and the judge and/or jury ultimately renders a verdict (evaluation). Similarly, a physician uses a variety of techniques to determine a patient's blood pressure, temperature, and overall physical condition (measurement), interprets those data based on medical science (assessment), and determines a plan for treatment (evaluation). If a patient disagrees with a physician's evaluation, he or she frequently seeks a second opinion, which also requires an evaluation.

The curriculum design evaluation strategy should use as rigorous a method of gathering, interpreting, and judging information as that used by the legal system and the medical profession as well as other professions involving human health and welfare. One way to ensure this is through the use of formative and summative evaluation.

FORMATIVE AND SUMMATIVE EVALUATION

Generally, formative evaluation is considered an evaluation of "work in progress" while summative evaluation provides a comparative analysis between or among curriculum designs to determine which is better/best. The purpose of formative evaluation is to make both the individual components and the total design as strong as possible. Summative evaluation shows whether the new design is better than what was done previously, better than other competing designs, or, in some cases, better than nothing (for example, having a sex education class versus not having one).

Because formative evaluation begins immediately at the inception of the design, it may include a formal assessment of needs, including societal and learner needs along with content/knowledge needs that must be addressed. Each design component should be evaluated individually to determine, for example, if the outcomes are age and/or developmentally appropriate, if the concepts, skills, attitudes, and beliefs are consistent with what learners need to know in the twenty-first century, and if the learning experiences are sequenced in a manner consistent with the structure and content of the curriculum. Finally, all the components are field tested in their entirety to determine if they function successfully together. This would be analogous to an automobile manufacturer testing a prototype car that has a variety of new components. Each component could be tested in a laboratory and found to be functioning perfectly, but the manufacturer could not conclude that the prototype worked successfully until it was driven extensively on a test track.

Although formative evaluation begins at a project's inception and may last one to three years, summative evaluation usually doesn't begin until between the third and the fifth year of the implementation. While this may seem to be a long time, remember that formative evaluation is an ongoing process that occurs while the curriculum is being designed and redesigned, and the summative evaluation occurs when the curriculum is complete and as strong as possible.

Because the summative evaluation is comparative, it is necessary to compare the new design with another design that addresses the same outcomes. Thus, it is possible to compare apples and oranges if one is comparing them as fruits. That would make it possible to compare a phonics-based language arts curriculum with a literature-based language arts curriculum if both were designed to meet the same reading and literacy outcomes.

A summative evaluation is in essence a "*Consumer Reports*" approach to comparing curricula. When *Consumer Reports* evaluates automobiles or lawn mowers or washing machines, it compares products that have virtually the same purpose, structure, and "content," and the same is true for a summative evaluation of curricula. Also note that *Consumer Reports* compares products and not the *users* of the products. Thus, when evaluating a curriculum design, it will be necessary to separate out the classroom teacher as a variable. A creative, enthusiastic, highly skilled teacher can "save" a poor curriculum, and an ineffective, boring, unimaginative teacher can "ruin" a strong curriculum. To not account for the teacher variable when doing an evaluation would be similar to making a Type I or a Type II error in a quantitative research study.

When writing an evaluation strategy for a curriculum design, the designer should:

1. Describe both the formative and summative phases of the evaluation strategy.
2. Indicate which techniques will be used in each phase (for example, test scores, interest surveys, attitude inventories, observations, interviews, needs assessments) and how the collected data will be used to help make judgments in each phase of the design.
3. Indicate which components of the design, if any, will receive particular attention during the formative evaluation because of special concerns specific to that component or components.

ACTIVITY 4.1

Establish groups of four to six educators in each group. Their purpose is to provide substantive critique and feedback on the following components of the design process and product:

- Statement of Purpose
- Concept map(s)

- Unit (subunit) identification and sample outcomes for each unit/subunit
- Sequencing rationale
- Evaluation strategy

---

4. Provide evidence that the summative evaluation will not be biased (that is, use measurements and assessments that an outside, "objective" assessor administers).

5. Make sure that the strategy has evaluated the curriculum design and not the teacher(s), students, and instructional activities.

REFERENCES

Eisner, E. (1979, 1985). *The educational imagination*. New York: Macmillan.

Eisner, E. (1969). Instructional and expressive objectives: Their formulation and use in curriculum. In W. J. Popham (Ed.), *AERA monograph on curriculum evaluation: Instructional objectives* (pp. 1–18). Chicago: Rand McNally.

Gagné, R., & Briggs, L. (1979). *Principles of instructional design*. New York: Holt, Rinehart, & Winston.

Mager, R. (1962). *Preparing instructional objectives*. Palo Alto, CA: Fearon Publishers.

Popham, W. J. (1969). *Instructional objectives*. Chicago: Rand McNally.

Posner, G. J., & Rudnitsky, A. H. (2001). *Course design: A guide to curriculum development for teachers* (6th ed.). New York: Addison-Wesley Longman.

Posner, G. J., & Strike, K. A. (1976). A categorization scheme for principles of sequencing content. *Review of Educational Research, 46*, 665–690.

5

Knowledge: Concepts and Facts in Context

Chapter 2 examined different orientations toward curriculum and in particular how these orientations placed knowledge, learner, and societal needs within the structure of the curriculum. Chapters 3 and 4 established the design product and the design process structurally and substantively. This chapter will analyze how essential concepts and facts, learners' attitudes and beliefs, and societal problems and expectations can be contextualized within the curriculum. The Statement of Purpose articulated in Activity 2.1 in Chapter 2 already provides some insights into the orientation toward the three sources of curriculum, but now it is necessary to specify what societal, learner, and content needs mean.

THINKING ABOUT CONCEPTS

No matter what content area, grade level, or developmental stage teachers are working with, they are constantly teaching concepts. Whether introducing a new concept (concept formation), practicing and applying a concept (concept development) or using a concept in context (concept attainment), concepts are the primary focus of both curriculum and instructional design. Unfortunately, although concepts are constantly taught, a thorough understanding of the essential elements of concepts, how concepts relate to each other, and how learners construct and assimilate concepts into their cognitive structure may be missing.

To test this assertion, try to complete the following activity that involves a preassessment of concept knowledge.

ACTIVITY 5.1   Identifying Concepts (Preassessment)

1. Given the curricular area you are planning to design or redesign, list at least 10 but no more than 20 major concepts that are essential for students to learn.
2. Group the concepts listed by a categorical relationship that links them together.
3. Organize those groupings by showing the superordinate, coordinate, and subordinate concepts in each category.
4. Finally, identify the attributes of each of the concepts in *one* of your categories to show how and where the superordinate, coordinate, and subordinate concepts share common attributes.

After completing this preassessment, you may feel confused, frustrated, or both. This is natural and may also reflect how students would feel if they were asked to perform the same task after completing a unit that has just been taught. Fortunately, there is a way to begin thinking about concepts and concept learning that will alleviate much of this confusion and frustration.

UNDERSTANDING CONCEPTS

Common cognitive activities such as problem solving, communicating thoughts and feelings, and organizing daily activities would be virtually impossible without concepts. The most generally accepted definition of the term *concept* is (a) a way to categorize and organize experiences and (b) a way to connect the web of ideas that emerge from the categorization (Martorella, 1990, p. 153). The organizational pattern(s) that concepts enable might best be compared to what a filing system does with data entered into a computer. Without a filing system in a computer, data retrieval would be incredibly time-consuming and highly frustrating. Similarly, without the schema that are formed through organizing experiences by concepts, anything above sensorimotor-cognitive activity would be virtually impossible (for example, a child stacking blocks).

To discover how concepts help organize experiences and ultimately patterns of thought, you need to understand the elements that make up concepts and how these elements can help organize conceptual structures for curriculum design. Peter Martorella has done one of the most thorough analyses of concepts, and his model provides a crucial piece for understanding concepts.

CONCEPT ATTRIBUTES

Each concept consists of attributes, and these attributes can be described as either criterial (essential to defining the concept) or noncriterial (nonessential for defining the concept) (Martorella, 1990, p. 152). Although the definition of a concept may contain both criterial and noncriterial attributes, it is from the criterial attributes that we derive examples when teaching the concept. To fully understand the concept, a learner must be able to distinguish between the criterial and noncriterial attributes and demonstrate how and why the criterial attributes fit that concept and that concept only.

For example, when you define an island as a body of land surrounded on all sides by water, the phrase "land surrounded by water" represents the criterial attributes (Martorella, 1990, pp. 154–155). Size, location, and topography of the island would be noncriterial attributes. If a learner confuses noncriterial and criterial attributes and concludes that an island is a body of land located in the ocean, for example, then that learner has formed a misconception. By the time students reach high school, they have managed to store a significant number of these in their memory in virtually every content area. In many cases, this is because the concepts and their attributes are learned out of context, and thus the student has categorized and organized the concept incorrectly. In extreme cases, as Martorella points out, these misconceptions can form stereotypes or faulty generalizations (1990, pp. 155–156).

Activity 5.1 required identifying concepts and organizing them based on some categorical relationship that depicted similar characteristics across all the concepts in that group. To complete this activity successfully, you would need to identify criterial attributes for the concept(s), separate them from the noncriterial attributes, and then categorize them through a pattern that linked superordinate, coordinate, and subordinate concepts together. So, if the list of concepts included *vertebrates,* for example, all subconcepts would show the same criterial attributes of having a spine with an internal skeletal system whether they were birds, mammals, fish, or amphibians. Noncriterial attributes would include the manner in which offspring are born, method of breathing, and external covering (fur, scales, feathers). If these distinctions were not made or if criterial and noncriterial attributes were cross-categorized, then it would be difficult to identify appropriate examples and nonexamples when teaching these concepts.

TYPES OF CONCEPTS

Martorella distinguishes four different ways to organize concepts by type: concrete/abstract, formal/informal, conjunctive/disjunctive/relational, and enactive/iconic/symbolic. The third category has the greatest implications for curriculum design (Martorella, 1990, pp. 157–159) because the conjunctive/disjunctive/relational pattern focuses on the criterial attributes and how these attributes define the concept.

Conjunctive concepts have one set of criterial attributes that define the concept, and these attributes (two or more) remain the same across all examples. In a dictionary, the conjunctive concept would most likely have one definition. Concepts such as island, mountain, and chair are generally considered conjunctive concepts. Even when another definition is given (for example, a self-service "island" in a gas station), the concept of island still maintains the same set of attributes. Rather than a body of land surrounded on all sides by water, however,

the island in the gas station is a raised body of concrete with gas pumps on it surrounded on all sides by asphalt. This is a metaphorical variation on the original
concept of island, but the essential, criterial attributes remain the same.

Disjunctive concepts consist of two or more sets of criterial attributes, all of
which must be taught with appropriate examples to ensure complete understanding of the concept. These concepts tend to have multiple definitions in a dictionary. For example, the concept of "strike" in the context of baseball is a
disjunctive concept. Besides ignoring the fact that strike already has multiple
meanings in other contexts (for example, bowling, labor disputes, lighting a
match), we must understand all criterial attributes of strike to fully grasp its meaning when applied to teaching someone to play baseball.

Thus, a teacher or coach would need to distinguish among a strike as a swing
and a miss, a foul ball, and a pitch in the strike zone that a batter fails to swing at.
Each of these has its own set of criterial attributes, and all are necessary to achieve
complete attainment and assimilation of this concept. Incorporating only one or
two of these alternative meanings into one's schema for baseball would create a
misconception.

The third type of concept, the relational concept, is the most difficult to categorize and hence to teach. This is because relational concepts may have one or
several sets of criterial attributes, but these attributes have no real meaning unless
they are viewed in relation to another set of attributes from another concept
(Martorella, 1990, p. 158). One way to characterize these concepts is that they
require perspective or multiple perspectives. Concepts such as freedom, justice,
love, and good taste are relational because they are totally dependent on context
to define them. For example, when does one person's discarded old toy become
a collectible for someone else? When does liberty become license and when does
a terrorist become a freedom fighter?

Content areas such as social studies and literature are fraught with examples
of relational concepts. Typically, there is no *one* correct definition. Problems arise
when teachers treat relational concepts as if they are conjunctive concepts. This
leads teachers to expect students to identify the "correct" meaning for a symbol
used in a poem, to interpret the author's meaning "correctly" in a short story, or
to define patriotism "correctly" when comparing revolutions in the United
States, France, and Russia. Relational concepts are clearly the most challenging
type of concept to teach. It is critical for teachers to identify the relational concepts within their content areas to avoid problems that occur when they are confused with conjunctive and even disjunctive concepts.

CONCEPT MAPPING

Concept maps were initially developed in 1972 by Joseph Novak and his colleagues at Cornell University, but they have become considerably more popular
since the early 1990s (Novak, 1998, p. 11). Basing much of its work on David
Ausubel's theory of meaningful verbal learning (1963), Novak's research group

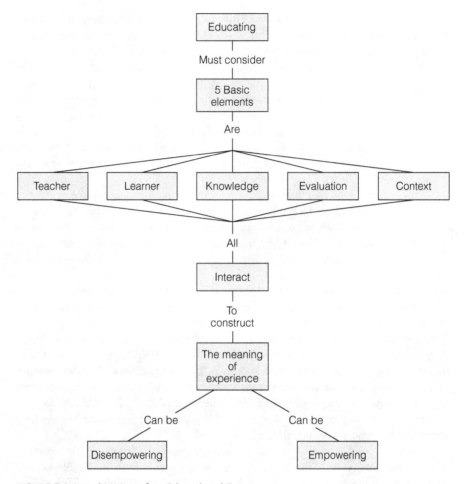

FIGURE 5.1 Novak's Map of an Educational Event

Source: From Joseph Novak, *Learning, Creating, and Using Knowledge*, p. 11, 1998. Reprinted by permission of Lawrence Erlbaum Associates, Inc.

sought to create a strategy to facilitate learners' assimilation (that is, development and attainment) of new and/or difficult concepts (Novak, 1998, p. 50) and to make the construction of new knowledge contextual and meaningful. This differs significantly from the rote memorization of concept labels that seems to dominate many classrooms (Novak, 1998, p. 19).

Although they appear to have similar characteristics, concept maps differ significantly from more familiar cognitive strategies such as graphic organizers and webbing. They more closely resemble the advance organizers postulated by Ausubel in his text on meaningful verbal learning (1963). Graphic organizers are designed to assist student learning because they are visual, thus helping visual learners; are static, thus helping learners who need consistency; allow students to reflect at their own pace; and present abstract information in a concrete manner (Myles & Southwick, 1999). Hierarchical organizers represent key ideas and subtopics in a linear form. Conceptual organizers take a topic or main idea and enable the creation of webs that move outward from the main idea. Sequential organizers follow a linear pattern such as a timeline. Finally, cyclical organizers structure events that have no clear beginning or end such as a water cycle (Myles & Adreon, 2001).

Webs are a subset of the graphic organizers and often look similar to a concept map because of the lines that connect the topics and subtopics and the way in which ideas are represented visually in circles, ellipses, or rectangles. However, webs tend to resemble exercises in "free association" where one idea triggers another idea or topic, thus creating a snowballing effect. Webbing facilitates such activities as writing or storytelling because they allow the student to represent sometimes random thoughts until a pattern appears.

Concept maps, however, provide a much clearer representation of the relationships between and among superordinate, coordinate, and subordinate concepts and, as noted earlier, they provide a clear pattern of criterial attributes if they're constructed correctly. Concept maps also tend to represent fewer concept terms than a web typically represents. This could make them somewhat less confusing, especially for younger learners.

Figure 5.1 shows a typical concept map, which includes Novak's five elements that make up an educational event (Novak, 1998, p. 11). Concept maps help provide a common set of terms that learners and teachers can share. They can be helpful in moving the learners from representational meaning to conceptual meaning. And finally, concept maps can help share the meanings of concepts and assist learners, even sophisticated ones, in constructing new knowledge (Novak, 1998, p. 38).

EXAMPLES OF CONCEPT MAPS

Although Appendix A contains examples of concept maps embedded within the sample curriculum designs created by K–12 educators, you should analyze examples specific to the major content areas to see how a map is constructed before trying to construct one. For example, the map in Figure 5.2 illustrates how the superordinate concept of "Living Things" might be depicted in a concept map designed for a fifth-grade science class.

Several features on this map are applicable to the other maps that will be examined. Initially, the superordinate concept is broken down into subordinate concepts of Animals, Plants, and Protists. In some science texts, five different kingdoms may be discussed, but in this particular case, the teacher chose to focus on the three kingdoms shown on the map. On this map, Animals, Plants, and Protists are considered coordinate concepts because they all represent different kingdoms of Living Things. Animals, Plants, and Protists are subordinate to Living Things, coordinate with each other, and superordinate to the categories below them (for example, Vertebrates, Invertebrates, Make Seeds). Thus, one particular concept may fulfill three different levels in a concept map.

In many cases, once the concept map moves beyond the second or third level of specificity, space for depicting the concepts becomes a problem. To facilitate

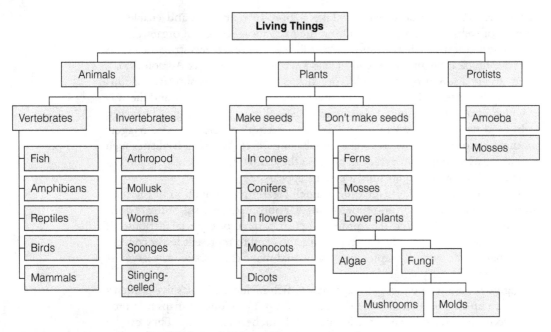

FIGURE 5.2 A Concept Map for a Fifth-Grade Science Class

the accurate depiction of the relationships among superordinate, coordinate, and subordinate concepts, it may be necessary to show concepts that would normally have a coordinate relationship vertically rather than horizontally. For example, in the concept map under Vertebrates and Invertebrates, the coordinate concepts of mammals, fish, birds, and so on are shown vertically rather than horizontally. To clarify these relationships accurately, the "boxes" (or circles or triangles) for the superordinate and subordinate concepts have the lines connecting them drawn into the top of the box

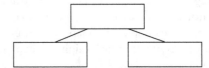

whereas the coordinate concepts have their connecting lines drawn into the sides of the boxes.

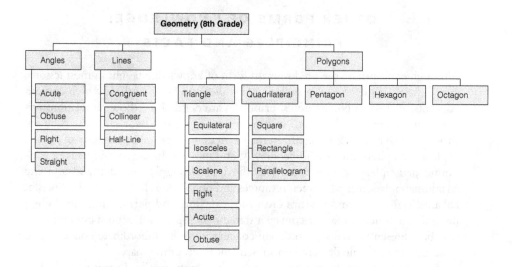

FIGURE 5.3 A Concept Map for an Eighth-Grade Math Class

This method of illustrating the relationships among concepts should provide clarity conceptually and facilitate the creation of the map pragmatically. There are several computer programs for creating concept maps, including Inspiration 7.0 or PageMaker.

The next example, in Figure 5.3, "Geometry," illustrates the other important features of concept mapping. This concept map, from an eighth-grade general mathematics curriculum, illustrates several important points to keep in mind when creating a concept map for a course, a unit, or a topic. A map represents the relationship among concepts as it did in the map on Living Things. However, it also illustrates what is going to be stressed primarily in the upcoming course, unit, or topic. In the Geometry map, several terms (acute, obtuse) occur in two different sections of the map, suggesting that these concepts will be revisited and reinforced later. The map also shows, however, that of all the polygons, triangles, and quadrilaterals are clearly the most important to study and retain because they contain significantly more subconcepts than any other polygon.

This example points out a critical issue when creating a concept that will be shared with students. When designing the map, determine if it accurately depicts the balance among the concepts that will be stressed in more detail and the ones that will be addressed more superficially. This will be particularly noticeable when assessing the extent to which learners have formed and assimilated the concept taught and if the assessment accurately conveys the degree to which essential concepts were stressed through instruction.

OTHER FORMS OF KNOWLEDGE:
PRINCIPLES AND FACTS

Although concepts are the predominant form of knowledge taught in most lessons, curriculum designs may also include principles and facts, both of which contain concepts. As Joseph Novak notes, principles are defined as "showing relationships between concepts." They "tell us how events or objects work or how they are structured" (Novak, 1990, p. 22). In the sciences, for example, principles of physics explain such phenomena as force, gravity, and motion. In the social sciences, economic principles are represented in the law of supply and demand and the Malthusian relationship between resources and population. In the arts, principles of balance, symmetry, and rhythm cross musical, fine, and performing arts. When designing a concept map to convey a statement of principle, the statement itself may be represented as a superordinate concept with the subordinate concepts that make up the principle depicted on subsequent levels of the map.

Facts are statements that have been verified empirically. In this regard, they indicate a valid record (Novak, 1998, p. 21). Facts also consist of concepts, and a factual statement may contain numerous concepts, all of which need to be understood. The factual statement that "water freezes at 32° F at sea level" contains at least four concepts (water, freeze, 32° F, and sea level). Problems occur when either a statement is presented as a fact when it is not valid or verifiable empirically or the concepts that make up the fact are misconceptions, contain noncriterial attributes as defining characteristics, or both.

Activity 5.2 provides an interesting approach to testing students' knowledge of facts that may actually represent misconceptions or misunderstandings.

ACTIVITY 5.2 Fact or Myth?

Next to each statement below, indicate whether you believe it is a *fact* or *myth,* and explain why you chose your response:

1. The three ships that Columbus and his crew sailed to the New World in or around 1492 were the Niña, the Pinta, and the Santa Maria.   Fact Myth

2. Vincent Van Gogh cut off his ear in his despair over a failed relationship with a lover.   Fact Myth

3. Abraham Lincoln wrote the Gettysburg Address on the back of an envelope while traveling to Gettysburg.   Fact Myth

4. America was named after Amerigo Vespucci.   Fact Myth

5. Crickets can tell the temperature.   Fact Myth

6. Johnny Appleseed really existed.   Fact Myth

7. In Salem, Massachusetts, witches were burned to death by religious zealots in the seventeenth century.   Fact Myth

8. The Emancipation Proclamation freed the slaves.   Fact Myth

9. The temperature at the Arctic Circle is not always below freezing.   Fact Myth

Although you may have responded to all the questions in Activity 5.2 correctly, this exercise does suggest that information is often expressed as factual when it is not. (The answers appear at the end of this chapter.) This occurs not only in classrooms but also through the media and other information-based institutions in society. These occurrences have been well-chronicled in books such as *Lies My Teacher Told Me* and numerous articles on myths and misconceptions in the sciences, history, mathematics, and statistics. The point is that when designing curriculum and instruction, the designer must be cautious in conveying information as factual unless empirical evidence supports such statements. This highlights the importance of context in teaching concepts, principles, and facts because all three depend on the contexts in which they occur to give meaning to them.

Following this discussion of concepts, facts, principles, and concept mapping, you should be able to create a concept map for the curriculum being designed or redesigned. Using the examples in Figures 5.2 and 5.3 in this chapter and the additional examples in Appendix A, try to create a map that shows superordinate, coordinate, and subordinate concepts for at least three but no more than five levels of categorization.

Go back to the responses to the questions in Activity 5.1 to help determine where clarifications, corrections, or revisions in the responses are necessary. It may also be helpful to re-examine the calendar-based curriculum map created in Activity 1.1 in Chapter 1. Be sure to maintain the levels and/or categories that accurately depict the manner in which the concepts were represented. When the concept map is finished, you should be able list 10 to 20 major concepts for the program, course, or unit being designed; group concepts together by the appropriate category (that is, conjunctive, disjunctive, relational); organize the groupings hierarchically (superordinate, coordinate, subordinate); and identify the criterial attributes of the concepts in at least *one* of the areas of the map. The successful completion of these outcomes should facilitate explaining the map clearly to other teachers, administrators, students, and parents.

REFERENCES

Ausubel, D. P. (1963). *The psychology of meaningful verbal learning.* New York: Grune & Stratton.

Jordan, D. (1993, 2001). *1001 facts somebody screwed up.* Atlanta: Longstreet Press.

Martorella, P. (1990). Teaching concepts. In J. Cooper (Ed.), *Classroom teaching skills* (4th ed., pp. 150–184). New York: D. C. Heath.

Myles, B. S., & Adreon, D. (2001). *Asperger syndrome and adolescence: Practical solutions for school success.* Shawnee Mission, KS: Autism Asperger Publishing.

Myles, B. S., & Southwick, J. (1999). *Asperger syndrome and difficult moments: Practical solutions for tantrums, rage and meltdowns.* Shawnee Mission, KS: Autism Asperger Publishing.

Novak, J. (1998). *Learning, creating and using knowledge: Concept maps as facilitative tools in schools and corporations.* Mahwah, NJ: Lawrence Erlbaum.

Answers to Activity 5.2

1. *Myth.* The Niña was actually the Santa Clare and the Santa Maria was La Galante. The Pinta's real name is unknown, but Niña and Pinta were nicknames given to the ships by the sailors.

2. *Myth.* Van Gogh cut off an earlobe, not his entire ear as the movies would have us believe!

3. *Myth.* Lincoln took more than two weeks to write the Gettysburg Address and finished it the night before in a hotel room in Gettysburg.

4. *Myth.* The name probably came from the Spanish word *Amerique,* which was a variation on a Native American word *Americ,* the name of a Nicaraguan mountain range.

5. *Fact.* If you count the number of chirps in 14 seconds and add 32, you'll get the temperature in Fahrenheit. Incidentally, only male crickets chirp.

6. *Fact.* John Chapman (Johnny Appleseed) really did plant apple seeds as a way to demonstrate his religious convictions that we should replace nature, not exploit it.

7. *Myth.* Nineteen were hanged and one crushed to death, but none were burned. Witch burnings occurred in Europe.

8. *Myth.* It promised freedom to slaves in rebelling southern states, but not in the northern states. Technically, it freed no one.

9. *Fact.* The temperature at the Arctic Circle can reach 90° F in the summer, and a variety of crops can be grown there.

SOURCE: Jordan (1993, 2001), pp. 2, 3, 10, 23, 47, 59, 72, 77, 123.

6

Connecting Outcomes
and Assessment

M ore than 30 years ago, John Zahorik examined the models teachers intu-
itively followed while planning their instruction. Despite the common
perception that instructional planning begins with determining the
objective(s) for the lesson, Zahorik (1972) discovered that teachers' first concerns
are with *what* they are going to teach the students. In other words, identifying
the content (key concepts and skills) occupied the teachers' attention initially
when planning for instruction. Although the lesson's objectives also ranked high
in the teachers' priorities, their greatest concern was with content issues.

Although this discovery may challenge our assumptions about priorities in
planning, it should not be terribly surprising. Given the even greater pressure
today to ensure that students have acquired essential concepts and skills as measured by state and national standardized tests, teachers today may be more preoc-
cupied with content decisions than they were 30 years ago. If outcomes are not
of primary concern among teachers as they plan instruction, then what role do
they play in the curriculum design process?

CURRICULUM OUTCOMES

In virtually all of the contemporary curriculum design models, educational outcomes (aims, goals, objectives, purposes) are depicted at or near the beginning
stages of each model and consistently precede decisions regarding content selection
and scope and sequence. This follows logically from the assumption that "you

can't plan a trip if you don't know where you're going." It also follows the progression of Ralph Tyler's four questions that guide curriculum design. This is where the curriculum design process differs somewhat from the instructional design process that Zahorik studied as he examined teachers' planning models. Curriculum designs tend to reflect an outcomes-based orientation to a greater extent initially than do teachers' instructional planning models.

This difference is largely due to the purposes of curriculum design, which, as Chapter 4 showed, are to connect outcomes, content, and assessment in a way that achieves *curriculum alignment*. Curriculum alignment will be examined in more detail later in this chapter, but essentially its purpose is to assess the gap between the intended learning outcomes (ILOs) and the actual learning outcomes (ALOs) to determine the effectiveness of the design components (Posner & Rudnitsky, 2001, pp. 8, 183). The curriculum is aligned if the students achieve the outcomes (as measured through a standardized assessment) at a level highly correlated with what the designer intended (Mertler, 2004). William Wraga, cited in Mertler (2004), suggests that this form of alignment ("front-loading") also has implications for assessing the effectiveness of formal instruction.

In the curriculum design process, curriculum outcomes usually emerge while the designer is trying to articulate a Statement of Purpose (see Chapter 2). These outcome statements tend to be general and bear little resemblance to the kind of "behavioral" or performance objectives teachers learned to write in their teacher preparation programs. Think of curriculum outcomes as an evolving phenomenon starting as very general statements that reflect how the curriculum will meet learner, societal, and content/knowledge needs. Eventually, the general outcomes will become more content and learner specific and will then be categorized for assessment purposes.

CATEGORIZING OUTCOMES

The first step in connecting outcomes with assessment for alignment purposes is to write clear general and specific objectives that reflect what students should be learning, not what they will be doing. As Eisner (1979, 1985) suggests, these objectives should be stated behaviorally (Type I objectives), focus on problem solving (Type II objectives), or allow learners to articulate what they have learned subsequent to a learning experience. Eisner (1979) calls these expressive (Type III objectives) objectives because the learner can express, through a variety of discursive (verbal or written) and nondiscursive (nonverbal performance) activities, precisely what he or she learned from the experience (or expressive encounter).

The curriculum designer chooses among the three types of objectives based upon the level of thinking, range of beliefs and attitudes, and degree of physical skill involved. As various models for categorizing outcomes are examined, examples will use each of Eisner's three types of objectives. As might be expected, different types of objectives work more effectively with lower-level cognitive, affective, and psychomotor learning experiences than they do with higher-level learning experiences. Looking at these models will also facilitate the selection of the appropriate method(s) of assessment for determining the extent to which learners achieved the desired outcomes. Generally, lower-level cognitive, affective, and psychomotor outcomes can be assessed effectively with observable, measurable, objective assessments, whereas higher-level outcomes require a greater variety of assessments involving performance-based, problem-solving, and contextual, authentic assessments.

Although numerous categorization schemes are available for grouping objectives, Bloom's taxonomy is probably the most familiar model for curriculum designers. However, we will also look at models developed by Robert Gagné and Leslie Briggs (1979) for categorizing "learned capabilities" in cognition, attitudes, and motor skills; and by George Posner and Alan Rudnitsky (2001) for categorizing skills (psychomotor-perceptual, cognitive, and affective), understandings (affective, cognitions), and affects.

Be aware, however, that these categorization schemes are helpful only insofar as they help connect outcomes with appropriate assessment strategies. Breaking learning down into cognitive, affective, and psychomotor domains is primarily an analytical exercise. In reality, neither teaching nor learning neatly separates into these domains. In short, the domain structures are fluid. It is difficult, if not impossible, to separate thinking from feelings, physical performance from the appreciation of that performance, moral development from cognitive development, and so on. Although an outcome may be categorized at a particular cognitive level, you also need to recognize the affective and sometimes the psychomotor dimensions of that outcome as you plan instructional activities and assessments.

Another important purpose for categorizing outcomes into levels is to determine if the balance among the levels is appropriate to the content being taught and the developmental level of the learners. Remember that balance does not mean equal amounts of each level. Rather, it means that the range and mixture of outcomes meets the societal, learner, and content needs identified. Just as a balanced diet doesn't mean eating equal amounts from each food group, a balanced set of outcomes doesn't imply an equal distribution of outcomes at each cognitive, affective, and/or psychomotor level. For an introductory course or unit in which the teacher is establishing a foundational base of information, one would expect a larger number of lower-level outcomes than in a more advanced, more complex course or unit. There is no magic formula for establishing the correct balance of cognitive, affective, and/or psychomotor levels in the outcomes selected in the curriculum design. As outcomes are assessed, the levels will be adjusted until an appropriate balance is achieved. The initial attempts at balancing the levels of outcomes will be largely intuitive, but ultimately, the assessment strategies will be the best guide for establishing a successful balance.

Bloom's Taxonomy as a Categorization Scheme

In the late 1950s, Benjamin Bloom and a group of colleagues established a "taxonomy" for categorizing outcomes in the cognitive domain to guide the development of evaluation strategies and models (Bloom, 1956). By 1964, David Krathwohl, Bloom, and others developed a related taxonomy for the affective domain (Krathwohl, 1964). Unlike scientific taxonomies, the categories were not mutually exclusive, but they were hierarchical in structure. That is, while there was some overlap across levels of the taxonomies with regard to how people think and believe, the levels were designed to build upon one another in each of the domains.

The levels in Bloom's taxonomy for the cognitive domain (1956) are structured as follows:

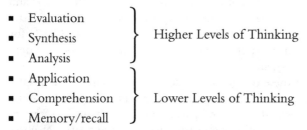

- Evaluation
- Synthesis   } Higher Levels of Thinking
- Analysis
- Application
- Comprehension   } Lower Levels of Thinking
- Memory/recall

For example, if the concept of *photosynthesis* were being taught, the teacher would structure the outcomes to reflect the level of thinking and write outcomes such as these:

- The student will be able to state the definition of photosynthesis. (memory/recall)

- The student will be able to explain the definition of photosynthesis in his or her own words. (comprehension)

- The student will be able to use principles of photosynthesis to grow and nurture a houseplant. (application)

- When given four separate plants that are not growing successfully, the student will be able to determine which aspect(s) of photosynthesis is lacking. (analysis)

- The student will be able to create a model depicting the process of photosynthesis as determined by the analysis of successful and unsuccessful plant growth. (synthesis)

- Using criteria established in the model of photosynthesis that the student created, he or she will be able to judge various approaches to growing and nurturing houseplants. (evaluation)

In these examples, a scientific principle and supporting concepts are learned hierarchically across all levels of cognition. The concepts are developed in a spiraling fashion with each level requiring more sophisticated thought processes. At each level, assessment would differ and become increasingly contextual as the depth and complexity of thought increased. Although lower levels of thinking (memory/recall, comprehension) could be assessed through easily measured, objective means, the higher levels (application, analysis, synthesis, evaluation) require more sophisticated, authentic, and, in some cases, more individualized assessment techniques.

The Krathwohl (1964) taxonomy for the affective domain follows a similar hierarchical pattern with some overlap of concepts across the levels. In addition, as one moves up the levels of the affective domain, it becomes evident that higher levels of cognition are also required. The affective domain is sequenced as follows:

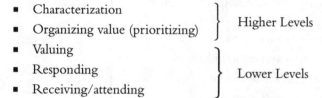

- Characterization
- Organizing value (prioritizing) } Higher Levels
- Valuing
- Responding } Lower Levels
- Receiving/attending

For example, if the concept of *participatory citizenship* is being taught, the teacher may emphasize the importance of being an informed, active, involved citizen. Hierarchically, the affective outcomes could be stated as in these examples:

- The student will actively listen to debates presenting different perspectives on a political issue. (receiving/attending)
- The student will present arguments supporting one perspective on a political issue. (responding)
- The student will develop a persuasive speech supporting his or her beliefs on a political issue and present it at a political rally in the school. (valuing)
- The student will examine a political issue from multiple perspectives and, after debating each perspective, defend one of them. (organizing/prioritizing values)
- The student will provide evidence of consistency of belief systems (that is, liberal, conservative, libertarian, and so on) in his or her own political position. (characterization)

In this example, the student is expected to show development of a belief system from simply being willing to listen to different points of view to being consistent behaviorally in representing his or her own sense of political agency. Clearly, this is not a process that evolves quickly, nor is it likely to be in evidence among younger children. One would expect, in the case of affective outcomes as characterized by Krathwohl et al. that the development of attitudes, beliefs, and values would take considerable time and a concomitant development of cognitive ability. Thus, teachers probably would link cognitive and affective outcomes closely together both in the way the outcomes are stated as well as in the way they are categorized.

The psychomotor domain is somewhat different and presents another set of challenges. Although Bloom's original group of educational psychologists did not develop a specific taxonomy for the psychomotor domain, R. H. Dave (1970), E. J. Simpson (1972), and Anita Harrow (1972) each devised a separate model for the psychomotor domain. Dave's model (imitation, manipulation, precision, articulation, naturalization) and Harrow's model (involuntary movement, fundamental movements, perception, physical abilities, skilled movements, nondiscursive communication) both seem to be incorporated into the model developed by Simpson. Simpson's model includes seven levels of psychomotor development:

- Origination (creates new patterns of movement)
- Adaptation (responds to unanticipated experience)   **Higher Levels**
- Complex overt response (shows skilled performance consistently)

- Mechanism (develops habitual responses)
- Guided response (uses trial and error/imitation)   **Lower Levels**
- Set (establishes a mental set for readiness)
- Perception (responds to sensory stimulation)

For a particular psychomotor skill such as *figure skating,* the outcomes could be arranged hierarchically as follows:

- The student will be able to maintain balance on a pair of ice skates. (perception)
- The student will be able to demonstrate the desire to perform figure skating movements on ice. (set)
- Following a demonstration by the instructor, the student will be able to perform the same movement(s) just demonstrated. (guided response)
- The student, after practicing, will perform simple figure skating movements consistently. (mechanism)
- The student will perform complex figure skating patterns correctly and without hesitation. (complex overt response)
- In a figure skating competition, the student will successfully perform a variety of complex skills that the judges require. (adaptation)
- The student will create his or her own figure skating performance following prescribed criteria. (origination)

In this example, the physical skill being developed becomes increasingly complex over time, as does the individual's level of proficiency. It is certainly possible that the individual could perform the skill competently but never reach the highest level of the taxonomy (origination). Note also that as the physical skill's complexity increases, there is a concomitant increase in the level of cognition and affective responses involved. By the time the individual reaches the level of habitual responses (mechanism), there is probably very little overt, observable thought occurring; the individual is most likely using higher-level thought processes instantaneously (for example, visualization and pattern recognition). The individual is also experiencing more intense and noticeable affective responses as well (for example, expressions of pleasure and pride in accomplishments).

The taxonomies that were developed by or evolved from the work of Bloom and his colleagues represent the most familiar models for most curriculum designers, but other options exist, such as those developed by Gagné and Briggs and by Posner and Rudnitsky. The next sections will explore these two models as ways of categorizing learning outcomes.

Gagné and Briggs's Learned Capabilities

Robert Gagné and Leslie Briggs (1979) provide another method for categorizing outcomes based on "learned capabilities" (Gagné & Briggs, 1979, p. 49). Although less well known than the Bloom et al. taxonomies, the model by Gagné and Briggs does make a stronger connection between how outcomes relate to specific functions of learning than the taxonomies do. As with the taxonomic levels, the learned capabilities also depict outcomes as representing cognitive, affective, and psychomotor functions.

Gagné and Briggs group the learned capabilities into five categories: verbal information, intellectual skills, cognitive strategies, attitudes, and motor skills. The first three categories represent cognitive outcomes, attitudes represent affective outcomes, and motor skills represent psychomotor outcomes in the Bloom et al. taxonomies.

Verbal information is the foundation of cognition. It consists of facts, labels, and terminology that can be recalled or accessed relatively easily from memory although not necessarily resulting from memorization (Gagné & Briggs, 1979, p. 50). Verbal information is necessary to perform higher-level cognitive activities because the learner uses the information (facts, terms, labels) to analyze and solve problems and critique differing perspectives. Ultimately, the learner organizes information into larger structures (Gagné & Briggs, 1979, p. 81) to facilitate the accessing and processing of that information (see Chapter 5 for a more detailed discussion of concept learning).

Intellectual skills help facilitate the processing of information at higher levels of cognition. They are numerous and, according to Gagné and Briggs (1979, p. 61), are increasingly complex when used in a hierarchical fashion. They group the most commonly used intellectual skills hierarchically in the following fashion (p. 62):

> **Problem Solving** (higher-order rules)
> *which requires as prerequisites*
>
> **Rules** (including defined concepts)
> *which require as prerequisites*
>
> **Concrete Concepts**
> *which require as prerequisites*

Discriminations

This model, based on Gagné's earlier work, *The Conditions of Learning* (1977), suggests that intellectual skills develop hierarchically from discriminations to problem solving. Discriminations involve being able to separate phenomena based on their characteristics (for example, colors, shapes, sounds, textures) (Gagné & Briggs, 1979, p. 63) so that concrete concepts can be developed using criterial and noncriterial attributes (see Chapter 5). Thus, according to Gagné and Briggs

(p. 65), a child may be able to identify a geometric shape (triangle) as different from another geometric shape (rectangle) by using discrimination, but not be able to identify the attributes of each as a concrete concept until those concepts are taught and used. Once those attributes are identified and used, the concept is then defined so that the learner can now separate a triangle from a rectangle, identify a three-sided figure and a quadrilateral, and then clearly define the attributes (criterial and noncriterial) to create an agreed-upon definition (p. 66).

In the Gagné and Briggs model, rules describe a regularity of performance in specific situations (p. 67). Rules, in this case, can be scientific principles, mathematical theorems, and linguistic rules that are empirically based (that is, the rules that govern the way sentences are structured in English, *not* spelling rules such as "*i* before *e* except after *c*"). Rules tend to be made up of and closely related to defined concepts so one must fully understand the concepts to truly understand the rule (p. 68). Higher-order rules provide the base for problem solving because effective problem solving usually involves applying several different rules or sets of rules across new or unanticipated situations or contexts. By connecting different rules or sets of rules, the learner is establishing higher-order rules to solve a problem (p. 70).

Cognitive strategies represent the highest level of cognition and are notable because they indicate *how* learners think—that is, using verbal information and intellectual skills—rather than recapitulating what they are thinking about. As such, cognitive strategies are not necessarily taught, per se, but instead, the teacher creates an environment in which the learner can use and develop his or her cognitive strategies (pp. 72–73). Examples of cognitive strategies include inductive and deductive reasoning, art, film, or literary criticism, and decision making. Although Gagné and Briggs's approach to learning is clearly behavioristic, it could be argued that their use of cognitive strategies suggests an early form of constructivist thinking whereby a learner is asked *how* and *why* he or she is thinking about a task in a certain way rather than being told *what* to think.

Using the Gagné and Briggs model to categorize outcomes in the cognitive domain is similar to Bloom's taxonomy. For example, the outcomes listed here could be categorized as follows:

- Given three-sided and four-sided figures, the student will be able to name triangles and rectangles. (verbal information)
- The student will be able to separate triangles from rectangles. (intellectual skill—discrimination)
- The student will be able to describe the attributes of a triangle and a rectangle. (intellectual skill—concrete concepts)
- The student will be able to compute the areas of given triangles and rectangles. (intellectual skill—rules/defined concepts)
- Using the Pythagorean theorem, the student will be able to determine the appropriate length of boards needed to support a retaining wall. (problem solving/higher-order rules)
- Using only triangular and rectangular shapes, the student will create an architectural design for an office building. (cognitive strategy)

The affective domain of Bloom et al.'s taxonomy does not distinguish among attitudes, beliefs, and values, but the Gagné and Briggs model regards *attitudes* as the major component of the affective domain (Gagné & Briggs, 1979, p. 85). Attitudes are actions that require a person to make a choice. An attitude is "an internal state which affects an individual's choice of action toward some object, person, or event" (p. 85). The key distinction that Gagné and Briggs make is that simply asking a person what his or her attitude is toward a particular phenomenon is insufficient. More important is knowing what course of action that person would follow based on the attitude he or she has toward that phenomenon (p. 86).

Attitudes are acquired either through direct experience or through indirect (vicarious) experiences, according to Gagné and Briggs (pp. 87–89). A person could acquire certain attitudes toward an ethnic group, social class, or race based on a series of intensive, long-term or short-term experiences with these groups or individuals within those groups. If questioned about why a person behaved a certain way when confronted with a situation involving a member of one of those groups, one would describe an action based on an attitude acquired through the direct experiences the person had.

However, people also develop attitudes indirectly through vicarious means. This usually involves some form of "human modeling" (p. 88). This is an equally powerful way to acquire a particular attitude because it usually involves a parent, a significant adult (for example, a teacher), a peer group, or a media image serving as a role model. As in the previous example, a person may have acquired strong beliefs about a particular ethnic group, social class, or race based not on any specific direct experience(s) but on what he or she saw or heard a significant role model do or say about that particular group. Given a series of these actions or statements over time, the person will acquire attitudes that will be as strong as if not stronger than those acquired directly (p. 89).

When writing outcomes reflecting the acquisition of attitudes according to this model, both direct and indirect experiences are emphasized, as the following examples show:

- Following 50 hours of service learning in a homeless shelter, the student will create an essay describing his or her beliefs about homelessness in the United States. (direct method)
- After interviewing parents, teachers, classmates, and clergy, the student will create an essay describing his or her beliefs about homelessness in the United States. (indirect method)

The final category in the Gagné and Briggs model is *motor skills,* which have three components: part skills, subroutines (sometimes called executive subroutines), and the total skill (Gagné & Briggs, 1979, pp. 90–91). Motor skills are essentially the same as the psychomotor skills discussed in conjunction with Bloom's taxonomy. Because they involve acquiring physical skill, motor skills require constant practice and corrective feedback until the skill is fully developed and internalized. As in the psychomotor taxonomy, motor skills are developed hierarchically, moving from part skills to the acquisition of the total skill.

Part skills are essentially the separate tasks that make up the total skill. If one is learning to drive a car, for example, the total skill of driving is broken down into the component parts of steering, braking, accelerating, turning, shifting gears, and so on, and the learner practices each part skill first either in a simulated context or in a relatively safe context. The trainer gives the novice driver constant and consistent feedback until part skills are demonstrated competently. In the case of motor skills, the old adage "practice makes perfect" is incorrect. In the case of part skills, "perfect practice makes perfect." Simply practicing the skills is insufficient. The trainer must give corrective feedback until each part skill is mastered.

Eventually, the part skills must be internalized so that performance becomes habitual. Integrating part skills involves the development of an executive subroutine (Gagné & Briggs, 1979, p. 90). Initially, when a learner is practicing a part skill, the thought processes involved in performing the part skills are obvious. Consciously thinking through the steps in the part skill, the learner performs relatively slowly and unevenly. Eventually, as a schema is developed and the part skills become integrated, performance becomes smoother and faster. Conscious thought becomes less obvious and eventually disappears. The novice driver, for example, develops what are frequently called "good driving habits" and consistently performs driving skills smoothly and quickly as the context warrants.

Finally, the learner acquires the total skill. Practice is useful primarily to keep skills sharp or to develop the skills more fully. The consistent performance of the total skill involves the correct sequencing of the part skills in each context where the total skill is necessary (p. 92). Performance is frequently assessed using a checklist of part skills that gauge the accuracy and efficacy of the overall performance (p. 92).

The examples of learning outcomes illustrating the acquisition of a motor skill indicate the important relationship among the three components: part skills, executive subroutines, and total skills. The following outcomes focus on the skill of driving a car:

- The student will be able to demonstrate correct procedures for turning a car to the right (or left). (part skill)
- The student will be able to demonstrate correct acceleration procedures. (part skill)
- The student will be able to demonstrate correct deceleration (braking) procedures. (part skill)
- The student will be able to correctly perform an evasive maneuver around a road hazard. (part skill)
- The student will successfully integrate the preceding part skills to demonstrate safe driving techniques. (executive subroutine)
- The student will successfully complete the road test required to receive a driver's license in his or her state of residence. (total skill)

Although similar to the taxonomies developed by Simpson, Harrow, and Dave for the psychomotor domain, the Gagné and Briggs model contains fewer components and thus may be easier to use for categorizing outcomes that involve learning motor skills. The broader categories in the Gagné and Briggs model, however, fail to account for the highest level in the Simpson taxonomy, that of original performance. The Gagné and Briggs model may be more useful when categorizing technical, mechanical skills, while Simpson's taxonomy may be more useful when categorizing artistic performance. Once again, the key is using the appropriate categorization scheme for appropriate content/context.

The Posner and Rudnitsky Model

George Posner and Alan Rudnitsky's model for categorizing intended learning outcomes incorporates the tripartite structure of Bloom et al. (cognition, affect, and psychomotor skills) while also introducing a somewhat simpler way of grouping all three domains under two headings: skills and understandings (Posner & Rudnitsky, 2001, p. 83).

The "skills" and "understandings" would be used to generate broad, usually nonbehavioral, general intended learning outcomes early in the curriculum design process. Later, these would be refined (p. 83) into more specific course or unit (subunit) level outcomes and grouped into four categories: cognitions, cognitive skills, psychomotor-perceptual skills, and affects.

Posner and Rudnitsky place cognitions and affects under the larger category of understandings and cognitive skills and psychomotor-perceptual skills under the larger category of skills (p. 88). Although both the taxonomic structures of Bloom and the learned capabilities of Gagné and Briggs are arranged hierarchically, Posner and Rudnitsky do not subdivide learning outcomes as specifically or narrowly. This allows designers to create their own prioritization of the four categories, but it also fails to provide the kind of specific guidance that some designers want or need for categorizing and prioritizing outcomes.

The approach that Posner and Rudnitsky use tends to represent cognitive, affective, and psychomotor learning in much the same way as the other two approaches, so the primary focus on their model will be how to use it to categorize outcomes.

Understandings

Under the larger heading of understandings fall the two categories of affects and cognitions. Affects are divided into affective skills and affective understandings. Affective skills are generally associated with some kind of behavioral manifestation of an attitude, belief, and/or value. These might include such skills as politeness, attentive listening, and social etiquette that represent an enactment of one's attitudes. These skills can be taught (p. 89). Affective understandings tend to relate to understanding one's self and others and may be an integral part of one's self-esteem, or self-concept. Although this type of understanding may have cognitive aspects, it seems to reflect a knowledge of one's own values or belief system and how that knowledge represents the essence of one's self (p. 89). Therefore, it is probably more of a "feeling" than a fact or a behavior.

According to Posner and Rudnitsky, "cognitions involve the incorporation or storage of information in the brain" (p. 93). Types of knowledge stored in the brain include facts, concepts, generalizations, and theories. For simplicity, these are referred to as "ideas" (p. 93). How one comes to acquire, use, and develop these ideas is reflected in the outcome statements for cognitions. Although not arranged hierarchically, the outcome statements written for cognitions should reflect the differing levels of complexity and abstractions involved in the study of facts versus theories, concepts versus principles, and generalizations versus laws. Ultimately, Posner and Rudnitsky describe cognitions in terms similar to those used by Bloom and others—such as memory, comprehension, and problem solving (p. 97).

Someone writing outcome statements following the Posner and Rudnitsky category of understandings (cognitions and affects) would create statements similar to those listed here. Please note that these are not arranged in any particular hierarchical order, which is consistent with their model.

Affects

- The student should be able to demonstrate appropriate behavior in a social situation. (affective skills)
- The student should be able to express his or her feelings about how adequately the social skills were perceived by others. (affective understanding)
- The student should be able to identify the "hidden persuaders" in a TV commercial. (cognition—comprehension)
- The student should be able to design an advertising campaign that successfully persuades a person to purchase a product. (cognition—problem solving)

Skills Posner and Rudnitsky divide skills into two categories: cognitive skills and psychomotor-perceptual skills (pp. 99–101). Similar to Gagné and Briggs's category of intellectual skills, cognitive skills involve a behavioral manifestation of cognition. In other words, the learner does something with what he or she knows. This is especially useful with contextual learning because the expectation is that information is better learned and retained if it is used in a "real" situation. Posner and Rudnitsky suggest that the teacher design a flowchart to accompany cognitive skills outcomes so that the learner knows how to demonstrate more complex, higher-order thinking skills (pp. 97–100).

Psychomotor-perceptual skills involve the demonstration of a physical skill and are similar to the taxonomy for psychomotor skills (Simpson) and the motor skills (Gagné and Briggs) discussed earlier in the chapter. Students use these skills in obvious areas such as physical education, as well as less obvious situations (for example, focusing a microscope, dissecting a frog, building a geodesic dome).

Examples of intended learning outcomes that focus on skills (cognitive skills and psychomotor-perceptual skills) include the following:

- The student should be able to analyze the major components of a short story. (cognitive skill—analysis)
- The student should be able to construct an original short story that uses the major components of a short story. (cognitive skill—organization)

MODEL 1 (BLOOM)	MODEL 2 (KRATHWOHL ET AL.)	MODEL 3 (SIMPSON)
Cognitive Domain	*Affective Domain*	*Psychomotor Domain*
Evaluation	Characterization	Organization
Synthesis	Organization	Adaptation
Analysis	Valuing	Complex overt response
Application	Responding	Set
Comprehension	Receiving/Attending	Perception
Memory/Recall		

MODEL 4
(GAGNÉ AND BRIGGS)

Cognition

Verbal Information	*Intellectual Skills*	*Cognitive Strategies*
Labels	Problem solving	Inductive reasoning
Facts	Rules	Deductive reasoning
Bodies of knowledge	Defined concepts	Critical thinking
	Concrete concepts	Decision making
	Discriminations	

Affect	*Motor Skills*
Attitudes	Total skills
Direct experience	Executive subroutines
Indirect experience	Part skills

MODEL 5
(POSNER AND RUDNITSKY)

Understandings	*Skills*
Cognition	Cognitive skills
Affect	Psychomotor-perceptual skills
Affective understandings	Affective skills

FIGURE 6.1 Five Models for Categorizing Learning Outcomes

- The student should be able to correctly demonstrate the four-step and the five-step approach in bowling. (psychomotor-perceptual—performance skill)
- The student should be able to demonstrate appropriate safety procedures when handling sulfuric acid and nitric acid in the chemistry lab. (psychomotor-perceptual skill—procedural skills)

Although, as noted earlier, the Posner and Rudnitsky model incorporates the elements of the other two models, it is somewhat simpler to use because of its more general, descriptive nature as opposed to the more specific, prescriptive taxonomic models and learned capabilities. Whichever model one selects for categorizing outcomes, it is essential to use that model consistently. (See Figure 6.1 for a summary of the three categorization models discussed in this chapter.) To mix or blend across the three models would be highly confusing, both conceptually and linguistically.

Before categorizing outcomes, be sure you address the following questions:

1. Do the outcomes focus on what students will be learning and not on what they will be doing?

2. Do the outcomes state what students will be learning and not what the teacher will be teaching?

3. Is the categorization scheme for organizing and prioritizing the outcomes clearly understood and are the outcomes labeled correctly and accurately?

4. Is the same categorization scheme used consistently for all of the program, course, unit, and/or subunit outcomes in the curriculum design?

If these questions are addressed successfully, the task of matching and connecting outcomes and assessment becomes much easier. Although the following section doesn't provide an exhaustive analysis of assessment procedures, it does discuss how assessment strategies can be selected to represent more effectively the outcomes being assessed and the context(s) in which those assessments should occur.

CONNECTING OUTCOMES
AND ASSESSMENT

Chapter 4 discussed the similarities and differences among the terms *measurement, assessment,* and *evaluation* in depth. Briefly, measurement involves collecting data to establish an information base for evaluative decisions. Assessment involves interpreting those data to provide meaning for them. Evaluation involves making a judgment based on the data and how the data are interpreted. The evaluation strategy that is created to determine the overall effectiveness of the curriculum design uses all three processes in varying degrees.

Because the major purpose of the evaluation strategy is to provide feedback on the extent to which learners attained learning outcomes and how much the curriculum design contributed to that attainment, both the data gathered and the interpretation of those data play a central role in the evaluation strategy. Selecting which data to gather and the conditions under which the data will be gathered is the first step. The measurement, or data gathering, techniques used tend to be dictated by contextual factors (for example, the age and cognitive developmental level of the learners, the type of content/skills being taught, and the structure of the learning environment) and directly correlated to the outcomes desired. Whether those data are gathered using quantitative or qualitative techniques or some combination of the two depends on the contextual factors along with the actual outcomes themselves. Curriculum designers must be careful not to choose a measurement technique (qualitative or quantitative) before determining what information to gather and why. The type of information needed should determine the technique, not the reverse. Too often, designers use qualitative measures to gather data and ignore important quantitative data because the qualitative measures provided deeper, richer data. Or, in the opposite vein, designers use quantitative measures to gather data because "the numbers don't lie" and quantitative measures often seem more indisputable or "objective." However, the aggregated data don't often allow for the individual stories that can be told using qualitative techniques. Ultimately, a blended approach will probably furnish the kind of balanced data needed, but, again, the contextual factors should determine this.

Earlier in this chapter, the importance of curriculum alignment was discussed. Typically, curriculum alignment means synchronizing the curriculum content with the appropriate assessment techniques (Mertler, 2004). However, outcomes must also be synchronized with the content and the assessment techniques for the curriculum to be truly aligned. Outcomes should articulate the level and type of learning expected. If the learner is expected to achieve an expert level of performance on a particular set of skills (for example, driving a car), but the performance is measured based on a paper and pencil test of knowledge of driving rules, then the outcomes, content, and assessment are out of synchronization. This suggests that the curriculum is not aligned properly.

The misalignment of desired outcomes, content, and assessment devices is a major issue in contextual teaching and learning. As noted at several points in this text, in learning, context is everything. This is particularly true when synchronizing outcomes, content, and assessment. Although not every outcome will require an authentic assessment technique, each outcome should be assessed, individually or collectively, in a context appropriate to the outcome and the content being taught. Lower-level cognitive outcomes might best be assessed using paper and pencil objective tests when clearly correct and incorrect responses are involved. Lower-level affective outcomes might best be assessed through observation of students' overt behaviors, such as willingly participating in a class discussion about a controversial topic. Lower-level psychomotor skill outcomes might best be assessed through observation and performance checklists of "skill drills."

Conversely, higher-level cognitive outcomes might best be assessed by extended response essays describing how a problem-based learning situation was analyzed and solved. A higher-level affective outcome might best be assessed through an extended observation and discussion of why a student chose a particular course of action when confronted with a moral dilemma. Finally, a complex psychomotor skill might best be assessed by an extensive performance-based portfolio, or a panel of expert judges, or a combination of the two.

In Activity 6.1, try to identity different types of authentic assessment techniques that you could use with the lower- and higher-level learning outcomes listed. The purpose of this activity is to demonstrate that different types and levels of outcomes and content require a variety of assessment techniques. However, the assessment techniques must also be authentic to the context in which the outcome is being achieved and to the desired content as well. Thus, if the content occurs in a context of problem solving, project base, or service learning, then it follows that the assessment should also be conducted within that context.

ACTIVITY 6.1 Identifying Authentic Assessment Techniques

	LEARNING OUTCOMES	AUTHENTIC ASSESSMENT TECHNIQUE
Cognitive	■ The student will be able to state the definition of photosynthesis. ■ The student will be able to explain the definition of photosynthesis in his or her own words. ■ The student will be able to grow and nurture a houseplant. ■ When given four separate plants that are not growing successfully, the student will be able to determine which aspect(s) of photosynthesis is lacking. ■ The student will be able to create a model depicting the process of photosynthesis as determined by the analysis of successful and unsuccessful plant growth. ■ Using criteria established in the model of photosynthesis the student created, he or she will be able to judge various approaches to growing and nurturing houseplants.	
Affective	■ The student will actively listen to debates presenting different perspectives on a political issue. ■ The student will present one perspective on a political issue. ■ The student will develop a persuasive speech supporting his or her beliefs on a political issue and present it at a political rally in the school. ■ The student will examine a political issue from multiple perspectives and, after debating each perspective, defend one of them. ■ The student will provide evidence of consistency of belief systems (that is, liberal, conservative, libertarian, and so on) in his or her own political position.	
Psychomotor	■ The student will be able to maintain balance on a pair of ice skates. ■ The student will be able to demonstrate the desire to perform figure skating movements on ice. ■ Following a demonstration by the instructor, the student will be able to perform the same movement(s) just demonstrated. ■ The student, after practicing, will perform simple figure skating movements consistently.	

ACTIVITY 6.1 continued

LEARNING OUTCOMES	AUTHENTIC ASSESSMENT TECHNIQUE
▪ The student will perform complex figure skating patterns correctly and without hesitation. ▪ In a figure skating competition, the student will successfully perform a variety of complex skills that the judges require. ▪ The student will create his or her own figure skating performance following prescribed criteria.	

ACTIVITY 6.2 Identifying and Labeling Unit or Subunit Outcomes

Based on the concept map(s) created in Chapter 5, identify the major units in the course(s) or subunits in the thematic or topical unit. Then complete the following tasks:

- Group the units/subunits in the order in which they will be taught.
- For each unit/subunit, list the major outcomes using an appropriate format for stating unit-level learning outcomes. Use the concept map(s) as a guide for determining major outcomes.
- After stating the outcomes for each unit/subunit, label each outcome by type (cognitive, affective, psychomotor) using *one* model (that is, Bloom, Gagné, & Briggs; Posner & Rudnitsky) and by level within each type. Be consistent throughout the labeling process.
- After labeling the outcomes, indicate the approximate percentage of each type and level and explain why this percentage represents an appropriate balance given the developmental level of the learners, the content selected, and the context in which outcomes will be achieved.

Aligning the outcomes, content, and assessment techniques begins with the identification and labeling of the outcomes in each unit or subunit in the curriculum design. Ultimately, the evaluation strategy will determine the degree of success of this alignment process. To begin this process, complete Activity 6.2 and use the results as the outcomes that will make up the basic structure of the units or subunits. These will then be sequenced using one of the sequencing patterns described in Chapter 4.

REFERENCES

Bloom, B. W. (1956). *Taxonomy of educational objectives: The classification of educational goals.* New York: Longmans, Green.

Dave, R. H. (1970). *Developing and writing behavioral objectives.* Tucson, AZ: Educational Innovators Press.

Eisner, E. W. (1985). *The educational imagination: On the design and evaluation of school programs.* New York: Macmillan.

Gagné, R. M. (1977). *The conditions of learning* (3rd ed.). New York: Holt, Rinehart and Winston.

Gagné, R. M., & Briggs, L. J. (1979). *Principles of instructional design* (2nd ed.). New York: Holt, Rinehart and Winston.

Harrow, A. J. (1972). *A taxonomy of the psychomotor domain: A guide for developing behavioral objectives.* New York: D. McKay.

Kratwohl, D. R. (1964). *Taxonomy of educational objectives: The classification of educational goals.* New York: D. McKay.

Mertler, C. A. (2004). Linking curriculum alignment and test scores. In C. Boston, L. Rudner, L. Walker, & L. Crouch (Eds.), *What reporters need to know about test scores* (pp. 1–21). Washington, DC: Education Writers Association & College Park, MD: ERIC Clearinghouse on Assessment and Evaluation (co-publishers).

Mertler, C. A. (2003). *Classroom assessment: A practical guide for educators.* Los Angeles: Pyrczak.

Posner, G. J., & Rudnitsky, A. N. (2001). *Course design: A guide to curriculum development for teachers* (6th ed.). New York: Addison Wesley Longman.

Simpson, E. J. (1972). *The classification of educational objectives in the psychomotor domain. The psychomotor domain* (Vol. 3). Washington, DC: Gryphon House.

Zahorik, J. A. (1972). Teachers' planning models. *Educational Leadership, 33*(2), 134–139.

7

∾

Key Models
for Contextual Teaching
and Learning

This chapter serves as a bridge between the process and product of curriculum design and the process and product of instructional design, which will be articulated in Chapters 8, 9, and 10. Contextual teaching and learning (CTL) has reinvigorated and embraced two models that can serve at both the macro-design level (program, school district) and the micro-design level (course, unit) to structure contextually based learning experiences for students. In addition, as Chapter 8 will show, these models also provide a basis for instructional designs that facilitate unit and lesson planning for a CTL classroom. These two models are problem-based learning (PBL) and service learning. The next section of this chapter will examine the historical and philosophical roots of PBL and service learning, and subsequent sections will describe the models in more depth. In subsequent chapters, as you construct teaching units and sub-subunits using the planning models provided, you'll reference the PBL and service learning models.

SOCIAL PROBLEM SOLVING IN CONTEXT

Since their inception, schools in the United States have been perceived as vehicles for educating children to become "good" citizens. In the Colonial period, that meant the sons (literally) of the wealthy who would ultimately become leaders in society, but by the 1840s, at least in Massachusetts and later across the entire United States, it meant mass public education. As waves of immigrants entered the United States, the social adaptation orientation of schooling largely concentrated on the "Americanization" of children and youth because schools represented the initial phase of creating a "melting pot" society. By the 1880s, as Lawrence Cremin notes in *The Transformation of the School,* a major emphasis in the schools was to prepare young people for the world of work, whether as a general concept or in particular trades (Cremin, 1964, pp. 23–53). Vocational education became a major focus of formal education as early as 1910, as the schools tried to meet the challenge of providing minimally educated (from today's perspective) workers who possessed the basic skills necessary to function successfully in a rapidly growing industrial society.

However, the goal of preparing young people for an industrial society led to sharp criticism from educational reformers who charged that "industrialism had dissolved the fabric of community" (Cremin, p. 60). Thus, community centers became the context for social reform as settlements such as Hull House in Chicago were created to offset the sense of disintegration and alienation caused by industrialization (Cremin, pp. 60–61). Jane Addams, the founder of Hull House, saw her work as socialized education that contrasted sharply with the narrow perspective schools had taken on (Cremin, p. 61).

Addams's community center concept viewed education as the need to develop skills while seeing work in the context of history, culture, and technology. Her intent was to enable children and adults to function successfully in an industrial society while also being able to aspire to being more than cogs in a machine (Cremin, pp. 64–65). Addams's curriculum was totally contextual, blending pedagogical reforms of progressivism with the reality of acquiring concepts and skills necessary to be a productive citizen. Although criticized for romanticizing education, she certainly made it more humane (Cremin, p. 63).

By the 1930s, the Great Depression had increased the emphasis on the school as a community for learning because traditional schooling seemed to have failed to provide society with educated people who could successfully grapple with the severe economic and social crises of that decade. In Flint, Michigan, for example, the Mott Foundation funded an experimental curriculum design that brought the school into the community and the community into the school. The intent of this program was to have the school function as a center for community learning for literally 24 hours a day, 7 days a week. Both parents and their children, as well as other members of the community, could participate in learning the formal curriculum (history, English, math, science, and so on) along with recreational and leisure time activities and hobbies. Both the certified teachers and community members served as "teachers" depending on the context, and children frequently learned new concepts and skills side by side with their parents. As with Jane Addams's Hull House, the Flint Community Schools became a formal structure for addressing the profound social problems of the day.

By the late 1960s and early 1970s, schools again became a vehicle for addressing significant social ills. Schools were expected to solve the problem of societal segregation by bussing children to desegregated schools, to reduce hunger through free and reduced-cost breakfasts and lunches, and to provide drug education, sex education, and parenting education to resolve a wide variety of social problems children brought with them to school.

Some schools responded by supplying access to a wide range of social and health agencies within the school buildings, while others sought to create "microsociety" schools that would enable students to experience directly the problems and issues facing society within the protected confines of the classroom.

As other countries threatened to overtake the United States industrially and technologically by the late 1970s through the 1990s, schools responded by increasingly emphasizing industrial competitiveness and technological superiority. Programs such as School-to-Work and TECH PREP and the restructuring of vocational schools into career and technology centers suggested that the integration of workforce-related concepts and skills into the "regular" curriculum was central to the mission of public education.

As pressures mount on schools to be the focal point for adapting to and reconstructing society, it is essential to keep this pressure in an historical context. Schools will always be in a position of reacting and responding to social needs and societal problems, and one of the more promising curriculum designs for integrating problem solving into meaningful contexts is problem-based learning (PBL). Along with its promise, however, there are also challenges, and we will explore these as we examine the PBL curriculum design model.

DESIGNING THE PROBLEM-BASED LEARNING CURRICULUM

As noted earlier, problem-based learning is hardly a new concept, but it has gained considerable attention recently due to its application in a variety of contexts, including online instruction, teacher preparation, medical training, and, of course, contextual teaching and learning. Some trace its beginnings to William Heard Kilpatrick's project method (Kain, 2003, p. 2) of the 1920s and see it as related to other problem-solving models, such as project-based learning, case study approaches, and cooperative/collaborative learning models. Kain, however, disputes these latter comparisons (Kain, 2003, p. 3), and sees PBL as more closely tied to John Dewey's notion that educative experiences are almost always rooted in everyday problems encountered by learners.

Essentially, PBL assumes that society needs individuals who possess a "fluid intelligence" (Eisner, 1979) that allows them to use information to solve problems rather than storing information that may or may not be useful. As Kain (2003, p. 5) suggests, as a result of using PBL, students become self-directed learners.

The PBL model enables learners to practice, over time, solving problems across a variety of content areas. It follows a series of steps that are similar to the scientific method but are applicable to a number of experiences that are not typically associated with the scientific method. According to Kain (2003, p. 19), the steps of PBL are as follows:

- Define the problem
- Seek information
- Generate options

- Select a solution
- Formulate/present the solution within the parameters of the problem
- Debrief your experience

In addition to being applicable across content areas, the PBL model can also be used by individual students or in group investigations. In either case, it is crucial that the problem be of sufficient interest and significance that its solution is worth pursuing personally, socially, and/or academically.

The design structure for a PBL curriculum is fairly well defined. As opposed to a problem-oriented curriculum where an entire course could consist of a series of program- or unit-based problems, PBL designs tend to treat the subunit level and are designated for particular individuals or groups. These subunits could last anywhere from one to five weeks (Ross, 1999, p. 29). In the PBL design process, the teacher and student(s) would devise or select a problem, determine the purpose for which the problem was selected, and identify the form in which the problem will be presented. They would then identify the resources needed to solve the problem and describe the processes that students will follow as they do their work (Ross, 1999, p. 30). Ross further supports the importance of selecting problems that teach key concepts and/or skills, are intrinsically interesting, are central to the content area, field, or discipline, and are typical of problems that learners will actually encounter (Ross, 1999, p. 31).

Problem-based learning, even in a well-designed structure, can have its challenges. Critics express concerns that learners will not encounter important concepts and skills if they aren't part of the problems being investigated (Margetson, 1991, p. 36). In equating PBL with "discovery" learning, they argue that PBL is time consuming, consists of many "false starts" that could confuse the learner, and might be frustrating to learners who are seeking a "correct" or simple solution (Margetson, p. 38). Indeed, all of these could happen if PBL is poorly designed, but they are not indigenous to the PBL model. These criticisms do suggest that the design of the PBL experience must be carefully constructed, appropriate to the content and context of the learning experience, and sensitive to the concerns that surround any design that is not teacher controlled and/or directed.

SERVICE LEARNING

Although aspects of service learning have been discussed in the literature since the late 1970s, advocates of service learning tend to see the late 1980s and 1990s as the period of its largest growth in K–12 schools and universities. In the late 1970s and 1980s, college students tended to focus more on personal and professional goals as the decade became characterized as the "Me" decade. To counteract this movement away from social problem solving, educators began to develop programs that stressed the importance of "giving back to" or "serving" the community.

Early on, the emphasis on giving back to the community drew criticism from educators who perceived the community service aspect of service learning as too closely associated with community service as a punitive device in the legal system or as a form of involuntary servitude. Schools that required service learning as a community-based activity often linked this service to graduation requirements. In other words, students had to fulfill a defined community service activity to graduate. Although the intention was to promote social consciousness, the implementation was viewed by some critics as heavy handed.

To balance this criticism, the label of service learning came to replace community service as a concept and an activity because it seemed to stress both the need for meaningful civic responsibility and the importance of learning from this experience. The balance between service and learning is evident in some of the definitions of service learning:

> Service learning is a credit-bearing, educational experience in which students participate in an organized service activity that meets identified community needs and reflects on the service activity in such a way as to gain further understanding of course content, a broader appreciation of the discipline, and an enhanced sense of civic responsibility. (Bringle & Hatcher, 1995)

and

> Service learning is a teaching method which combines community service with academic instruction as it focuses on critical, reflective thinking and civic responsibility. Service learning programs involve students in organized community service that addresses local needs while developing their academic skills, sense of civic responsibility and commitment to the community. (Campus Compact, 2002)

Both of these definitions make clear that service learning must be linked with course content and have an academic and a community service orientation. To illustrate this balance more graphically, Eyler and Giles (1999, p. 5) cite Sigmon's (1996) categories of service learning in tabular form (see Table 7.1).

As Sigmon's model suggests, the ideal curriculum design would have a SERVICE-LEARNING orientation so the learner understands civic responsibility from the service activity while also transferring and applying concepts and skills learned in the school-based curriculum to the community-based activity. Because of the contextual nature of service learning, it is an ideal structure for contextual teaching and learning.

According to the Campus Compact Syllabi Project (2001), there are four basic principles to follow when designing a service learning course:

Engagement: Does the service component meet a public good? How do you know this? Has the community been consulted? How? How have classroom-community boundaries been negotiated and how will they be crossed?

Reflection: Is there a mechanism that encourages students to link their service experience to course content and to reflect upon why the service is important?

Table 7.1 A Service and Learning Typology

Service—LEARNING	Learning goals primary; service outcomes secondary
SERVICE—Learning	Service outcomes primary; learning goals secondary
Service—Learning	Service and learning goals separate
SERV—LEARNING	Service and learning goals of equal weight; each enhances the other for all participants

---

ACTIVITY 7.1 Should I Design a PBL or a Service Learning Curriculum?

Before you decide to design a problem-based or service learning curriculum, answer the following questions:

1. Does this particular course or unit lend itself to a PBL or service learning approach?
2. Does my teaching style support and am I comfortable with a PBL or service learning approach?
3. Have I or will I be able to identify problems or service projects that learners will find personally meaningful and socially valuable?
4. Is there sufficient time in the curriculum to incorporate PBL or service learning?
5. Are there sufficient resources to make the learning experience worthwhile?

Reciprocity: Is reciprocity evident in the service component? How? Reciprocity suggests that every individual, organization, and entity involved in the service learning functions as both a teacher and a learner.

Public Dissemination: Is service work presented to the public or made an opportunity for the community to enter into a public dialogue? For example: Do oral histories students collect return to the community in some public form? Is [sic] the data students collect on the saturation of toxins in the local river made public? How? To whose advantage?

In designing a service learning curriculum, the questions posed by the Campus Compact Syllabi Project offer an excellent starting point for articulating the purpose of the course, its major outcomes, unit objectives, organizational structure and content, and the strategy for evaluating its effectiveness. Social studies/social science-oriented courses would seem to be the most logical content base for a service learning component. There are also ample opportunities for service learning across disciplines and subject areas as well. As noted throughout the discussion of service learning, whatever community-based activities are chosen should have input from the community to be served, should apply and reinforce the content being learned, and should result in the attainment of meaningful learning outcomes.

Both problem-based learning and service learning challenge the curriculum designer and the teacher. Although they are a rich source for contextual teaching and learning, they also require considerably more time than traditional classroom-based learning experiences. Finding appropriate problems and service activities that are personally meaningful and educative to the learners as well as socially valuable can be difficult, especially in rural or isolated areas. Finally, because the teacher serves more as a facilitator and guide, he or she will need to have a trusting relationship with the students to empower them to investigate and address community-based problems and issues.

The responses to the questions in Activity 7.1 must be an unequivocal YES before beginning the design process. Both PBL and service learning have the potential for being powerful, rich learning experiences with numerous long-term benefits for students, but they must be done well and under the appropriate conditions.

REFERENCES

Bringle, R., & Hatcher, J. (1995, Fall). A service learning curriculum for faculty. *The Michigan Journal of Community Service Learning,* pp. 112–122.

Campus Compact Syllabi Project. (2002). Retrieved December 5, 2003, from http://www.compact.org/syllabi

Cremin, L. (1964). *The transformation of the school.* New York: Vintage Books.

Eisner, E. (1979). *The educational imagination.* New York: Macmillan.

Eyler, J., & Giles, D. E., Jr. (1999). *Where's the learning in service learning?* San Francisco: Jossey-Bass.

Kain, D. L. (2003). Problem-based learning for teachers, grades 6–12. Boston: Allyn & Bacon.

Margetson, D. (1991). Is there a future for problem-based education? *Higher Education Review, 23*(2), 33–47.

Ross, W. H., Lawrence, L. W., Dick, R., Roane, D., Schulte, M., Olivier, K., et al. (1999). Implementation of a new course with a focus on active learning through integrated curricular approach: Pharmacy care laboratory I. *Journal of Pharmacy Teaching, 7*(2), 15–34.

Sigmon, R. (1996). The problem of definition in service-learning. In R. Sigmon et al., *The journey to service learning.* Washington, DC: Council of Independent Colleges.

Designing Instruction for Contextual Teaching and Learning

8

Creating Instructional Units for Contextual Teaching and Learning

This chapter furnishes a transition from curriculum design to instructional design for contextual teaching and learning. The focus of this transition will be moving from *what* is being taught to *how* to teach, or from content in context to methodology in context. Because teachers rarely have total control of the curriculum, or what is taught, their curriculum design decisions tend to involve issues of either content prioritization and emphases or the organization and structure of learning experiences, outcomes, and assessment.

However, instructional design involves decisions about how to teach. It closely reflects a teacher's personal philosophy, style, and belief system about teaching and learning and how to construct learning environments. Thus, instructional decisions appear to be much more within a teacher's control and more likely to involve choices whose consequences are almost immediately evident. Instructional design is also an area in which teachers feel comfortable largely because of experience and teacher preparation programs that emphasize pedagogical and methodological theory and practice much more than curricular theory and practice.

The unit and lesson design models in this chapter should fit easily in most teachers' "comfort zones," at least in their basic structure. However, the lesson planning models recommended for use in contextual learning environments may be less familiar and will require some adaptation to fit each teacher's style. These include models for project-based and problem-based learning, the 5-E Model, service-learning models, and cooperative learning models. Although these models use elements of the basic lesson planning model that will be discussed later, the variations are significant enough to warrant a separate analysis of each one.

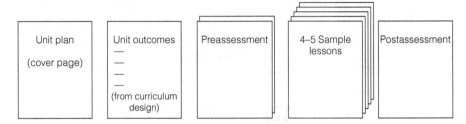

FIGURE 8.1 Instructional Design Conceptual Map

In preparation for planning the teaching unit or subunit, it may be easier to conceptualize the final product using a visual representation of the major components (see Figure 8.1). Give the unit or subunit plan a title that represents the major topic, concept, skill, or theme for easy reference and organization. Put this title on a cover page. Take the unit outcomes, already been completed in the curriculum design, and transpose them, with the appropriate categorization, to the instructional design. Each unit or subunit needs a presassessment and a postassessment so that the teacher can determine the extent to which each student reached the intended outcomes for the unit. More will be said about the actual structure of pre- and postassessments later, but at this point, note the importance of assessment in planning instruction.

The lesson plans represent the major component of the unit or subunit. Because a unit or subunit can typically last anywhere from one week to six weeks, there may be as few as 5 or as many as 30 discrete lesson plans. Some plans may span several days; you don't need to determine the exact number of lesson plans before beginning to design the lessons. To receive feedback from colleagues, classmates, supervisors, and instructors, etc., first develop four or five sample, prototypical lesson plans. These sample lessons should represent the range of strategies and/or models that will be used throughout the instructional design and should also represent various time frames (beginning, middle, and end) of the unit or subunit. The actual structure for the range of lesson plans will be discussed later in the chapter.

USING BEHAVIORIST
OR CONSTRUCTIVIST APPROACHES
TO UNIT/LESSON PLANNING

Since the early 1970s, research on effective teaching has focused on teacher behaviors and how they affect student learning. Beginning with the highly influential studies by Barak Rosenshine and Norma Furst (Rosenshine & Furst, 1973), researchers identified such key variables as clarity, enthusiasm, and variability as essential to effective teaching. Subsequent studies by Donald Cruickshank (Cruickshank, Jenkins, & Metcalf, 2003), Carolyn Evertson (Evertson, 1982), and Jere Brophy and Thomas Good (Brophy & Good, 1973) among others further refined and defined the teachers' behaviors most closely associated with increased student achievement and successful classroom management. More recently, the Educational Testing Service (ETS) has developed a model based on much of this research for its Praxis III/Pathwise training for evaluating effective classroom teaching. As a result, several states and many universities are using this model as a basis for preparing teachers and assessing successful classroom teachers at both the preservice and entry-level stages of teaching.

This research base has allowed educators to argue, with some confidence, that we now know more about effective teaching than we have ever known before. This level of confidence has probably contributed to the "No Child Left Behind" legislation policy makers arguing that only "scientifically based" research should be used to justify changes in curriculum and instruction in schools in the United States (No Child Left Behind, 2003). The more than 30 years of research on effective teaching has certainly provided an impressive basis for instructional decision making, but is it the only perspective on teaching and learning that should influence teachers' planning?

In the past 15 years, math and science education has emphasized constructivist research and theory, and this perspective has begun to influence other content areas. Indeed, much of the philosophy supporting contextual teaching and learning draws heavily from the constructivist paradigm (CTL, 1998). Based in the writings and practice of Dewey (social construction), Piaget (mathematical and scientific construction), and Vygotsky (language construction), this paradigm argues that learning is based on the individual's construction of understanding and meaning from experience (Disney Learning Partnership, 2002). Learning is powerfully affected by prior experience, perceptions of relevance to self and society, and the context in which learning occurs. Thus, advocates for CTL see the constructivist paradigm as the strongest explanation for why contextual teaching and learning works (Howey, 1998).

Although constructivists acknowledge that students are constructing knowledge in a traditional classroom, they see the major difference as being one of emphasis. That is, in a traditional classroom, the emphasis is on the teacher's behavior while in the constructivist classroom, it's on the learner's perceptions (Disney Learning Partnership, 2002).

Obviously, based on the comparison in Table 8.1, the constructivist classroom appears to be a much more desirable place to learn. However, classrooms are generally more complex, multilayered environments that rarely lend themselves to the kinds of distinctions drawn in Table 8.1. How can the behaviorist and constructivist perspectives be incorporated into contextual instructional design so that meaningful learning can occur?

Earlier, this chapter referred to the research literature on effective teaching, often dominated by studies on teachers' behaviors. Another body of research literature, primarily qualitative in nature, began to emerge in the 1980s and 1990s. This research focused on teachers' belief systems, arguing that how teachers constructed their own personal theories of teaching and learning played as large a role as their behaviors in determining effective classroom practices. Researchers

Table 8.1 Comparison of Traditional and Constructivist Classrooms

Traditional Classroom	Constructivist Classroom
Curriculum begins with the parts of the whole. Emphasizes basic skills.	Curriculum emphasizes big concepts, beginning with the whole and expanding to include the parts.
Strict adherence to fixed curriculum is highly valued.	Pursuit of student questions and interests is valued.
Materials are primarily textbooks and workbooks.	Materials include primary sources of material and hands-on activities.
Learning is based on repetition.	Learning is interactive, building on what the student already knows.
Teachers disseminate information to students; students are recipients of knowledge.	Teachers have a dialogue with students, helping students construct their own knowledge.
Teacher's role is directive, rooted in authority.	Teacher's role is interactive, rooted in negotiation.
Assessment is through testing, correct answers.	Assessment includes student works, observations, and points of view, as well as tests. Process is as important as product.
Knowledge is seen as inert.	Knowledge is seen as dynamic, ever changing with our experiences.
Students work primarily alone.	Students work primarily in groups.

such as Bullough and Gitlin (1995), Connelly (1988), Clandinin (1986), Britzman (1991), and Ayers (1993) persuasively argued that to understand good teaching one must understand how teachers put their belief systems into practice. Effective teachers not only exhibited behaviors associated with effective teaching but also understood and could articulate why certain behaviors worked under certain conditions and why others didn't. In other words, they understood the contextual nature of the teaching profession. What is effective with one class, one year, in one location may be totally ineffective if any of those contextual variables change.

It is becoming increasingly evident that teachers' instructional decisions must account for phenomena that are both behaviorist and constructivist in their philosophical origin. In a first-grade classroom at the start of the school year when the teacher is trying to establish the appropriate behaviors for entering and exiting the classroom, a social learning (modeling) strategy (Bandura, 1977) would probably represent effective teaching. In a fifth-grade math class in which the students consistently used inappropriate strategies for solving story problems, the teacher would most likely use a constructivist teaching strategy to determine why students had difficulty thinking through the problem in the story. Finally, in a high school literature class, a teacher might use a "blended" strategy for teaching *The Catcher in the Rye* by having students describe the literary elements of plot, theme, and narrative voice before having them identify their own unique meanings for the symbol of the catcher in the rye based on their experiences as adolescents. The balance between using effective behaviorist teaching strategies and effective constructivist teaching strategies is not so much an issue of right and wrong strategies as it is an issue of better and worse choices depending on the context.

BASIC AND ALTERNATIVE MODELS
FOR INSTRUCTIONAL PLANNING

Chapter 9 will examine the phases of instructional design as they relate to constructivist and behaviorist theory and practice, but first we need a description of basic and alternative models for lesson planning. Experienced teachers may have long ago stopped writing extended lesson plans with detailed descriptions of outcomes, assessments, and activities. As noted in Chapter 4, teachers' planning models usually focus on what is to be learned in a given lesson followed by selecting appropriate outcomes and learning activities (Zahorik, 1975). In most cases, these elements are noted briefly in a "block" lesson plan and then referred to only sporadically during instruction.

However, formal instructional design requires a well-articulated written plan that indicates the concept or skill to be taught, key objective(s), procedures that will introduce, develop, and apply the concept or skill, and a description of formal or informal assessment strategies that will be used during and/or after the formal lesson. This provides the teacher and anyone evaluating the effectiveness of the teaching episode with a point of reference by which to connect the teacher's intended learning outcomes with student learning, or *actual* learning outcomes (Posner & Strike, 2002). Although this may seem to be an unnecessarily time-consuming and complicated activity for the experienced teacher, it greatly facilitates the reflective-analytic assessment process for determining whether a teaching episode is effective on a daily basis or collectively at the end of a unit. Once units have been designed and then taught several times, the process becomes one of fine tuning rather than one of making major changes each day.

The basic lesson planning model in Figure 8.2 outlines the steps just described and provides a common point of departure for the alternative lesson planning models presented later. Chapter 9 discusses the steps in the basic model more extensively when it examines the stages of instructional design.

A basic lesson plan is generally used for a one-day lesson of 45 to 90 minutes, but it can be expanded by extending the activities described in the procedures to a second or even third day. However, even with an expanded plan, there will still be well-defined introductory, developmental, and concluding activities whenever there is a gap in time between lessons.

In the initial stages of lesson planning, the *content* and *outcomes* will have already been identified during the curriculum design. The content will come from the concept map or skills flowchart developed in Chapter 5. The lesson objectives will be more specific, refined versions of outcome statements identified and labeled in Chapter 6 and organized in Chapter 4. These lesson objectives will be behavioral, problem solving, or expressive, depending on the content, the experiential background of the learner, and the context in which learning will occur.

The *procedures* will describe activities designed to introduce the concept or skill to the learners (approximately 5 to 10 minutes in a 45-minute lesson), develop the concept of skill through examples and discussion questions related to them (about 25 to 35 minutes in a 45-minute lesson), and conclude the lesson by

Title of Lesson

I. Concept or Skill to Be Learned (Content)
II. Lesson Objective(s)
III. Procedures
    A. Introductory Activity
    B. Developmental Activity
    C. Concluding Activity
IV. Assessment/Evaluation Strategy
V. Materials/Resources (if needed)

FIGURE 8.2 The Basic Lesson Planning Model

reviewing or summarizing the concept or skill (5 to 10 minutes in a 45-minute lesson). These descriptions will contain some detail but the total lesson plan should be no longer than one to two pages maximum.

The *assessment* or *evaluation* stage of the lesson plan will describe strategies embedded in the lesson so that assessment is ongoing and continuous and will contribute to an overall evaluation strategy for determining if students actually reached the desired objective(s). These strategies could range from informal observations to a performance check sheet to a formal quiz, depending on the context in which the concept or skill is learned.

Finally, identify any *materials* or *resources* to be used in the lesson prior to instruction. This stage is crucial if materials (videos, DVDs, lab equipment) or resources (outside speakers, field sites) will be needed in the lesson. Not every lesson will require materials or resources, however, so this stage of the lesson plan is optional.

The 5-E Learning Cycle Model

Although the basic lesson planning model that Figure 8.2 outlines is highly serviceable and adaptable to any number of content areas and contexts, more specific models have been developed for particular content areas and types of learning experiences. One of these, the 5-E Learning Cycle Model, has been used successfully in science, mathematics, and social studies classrooms from kindergarten through college. The Biological Sciences Curriculum Study developed this model, which has been in the literature since 1966. However, it has become an integral part of science and math methodology courses only recently, primarily due to its strong linkage to constructivist theories of teaching and learning. It is also highly adaptable to contextual teaching strategies whether for a one-day lesson or for lessons that span several days.

The basic components of the 5-E Learning Cycle Model are *engage, explore, explain, extend,* and *evaluate*. As described on the Maryland Virtual High School website (November 20, 2003), the five steps in the model incorporate the following teacher and student behaviors.

- *Engagement:* activities that capture students' attention, stimulate their thinking, and help them access prior knowledge.

Title of Lesson

I. Concept or Skill to Be Learned
II. Lesson Objective(s)
III. Procedures

Phase	Description of Activity
Engagement	Describe activity or activities that will capture students' attention, introduce the concept or skill, and link the concept or skill with students' prior knowledge and experience.
Exploration	Describe activity or activities that will help students to plan, investigate, and organize the information they have collected.
Explanation	Describe process by which students will analyze information they found in their exploration. Describe reflective activity(ies).
Extension	Describe context or concepts that will allow students to apply what they learned to extend their understanding.
Evaluation	Describe assessment criteria and tools on how students will create their own assessment.

IV. Materials and Resources

FIGURE 8.3 5-E Learning Cycle Model Lesson Plan Format

Source: Maryland Virtual High School (2003).

- *Exploration:* giving students time to think, plan, investigate, and organize collected information.

- *Explanation:* students analyze what they found in their exploration. Their understanding should be clarified and modified through reflective activities such as journals, small-group discussions and self-evaluations.

- *Extension:* allowing students to expand and solidify understanding of a concept or skill by applying it to a real-world situation.

- *Evaluation:* students use an assessment tool or rubric provided by the teacher or create their own assessment to evaluate their level of understanding of the concept or skill.

To relate the 5-E Learning Cycle Model to the basic lesson plan model in Figure 8.2, engagement would occur during the introductory phase of the lesson; exploration, explanation, and extension would occur during the developmental phase; and evaluation would occur at the lesson's conclusion. Because the 5-E lesson would probably cover several days, however, it would probably be easier to design the lesson plan following the structure that Figure 8.3 depicts rather than using the basic lesson plan model in Figure 8.2.

Within the lesson plan format described in Figure 8.3, it would be useful to identify the approximate amount of time allocated to each phase of the 5-E Model. This is especially important when the lesson spans several days and the students are working on their own or in small groups to complete the activities. Because the teacher's role in the 5-E Learning Cycle Model is one of a guide or facilitator, a defined time frame for each phase of the model will help keep students on task and provide a concrete reference point for completing the task.

The Service Learning Model

Another planning model that is central to contextual teaching and learning is the service learning model. Although related to both the problem-based and project-based models that will be discussed later, the service learning model is more general and tends to incorporate elements of both project- and problem-based approaches. This is because service learning itself usually involves a major project designed to address some community-based problem. These could include such disparate problems as homelessness, adult illiteracy, environmental pollution, and voter apathy. Usually these projects cross content areas and incorporate issues related to economics, scientific inquiry, language skills, and statistical analyses of survey data.

Sometimes, however, service learning projects overemphasize the service component and fail to integrate important learning outcomes. This suggests that essential elements of John Dewey's theory of experience have been overlooked. As noted in that theory, not all experiences are educative and, in fact, some experiences can be mis- or noneducative if only done for the sake of the experience. For example, serving homeless families in a soup kitchen may fail to engage students in reflecting upon the economic and social conditions in the United States that require service organizations to run soup kitchens. Thus, the critical nexus of action and reflection in Dewey's theory of experience is lost in experiencing the interaction with homeless people in a soup kitchen.

This example points out the need to balance the concept of *service* with the concept of *learning* as discussed in Chapter 7. The design of service learning units and lessons must include a component after service learning that engages the students in a reflective analysis of what they experienced and how that relates to their research findings and larger issues of equity, justice, power, and influence.

Most service learning projects can run anywhere from two or three days to six weeks to an entire semester. The length of the project will relate to such variables as the nature of the problem being addressed, the availability of resources to conduct the service learning project successfully, the age and developmental/experiential level of the students, and the necessity for completing the service learning project in its entirety. For example, if the project involves building a home through a joint effort with Habitat for Humanity, the project is finished when the house is completed. However, if the project involves cleaning up a local river, the project may never be completed because new pollution may be added to the river virtually every day. Clearly, the reflective analysis in both examples should involve a discussion of what it means to solve a problem and complete a service learning task.

The unit plan for a service learning project will involve a series of lessons that establish the importance of reflection and analysis of the experience after the service learning (see Figure 8.4). Also note the amount of time to be spent on each stage of the process. Finally, both formative and summative assessments should be designed to determine what students are learning throughout the project and as a result of participating in the project.

Service learning requires a teacher who sees himself or herself as a facilitator or guide for learning rather than as a source of information. Not every teacher can or should use service learning as a major component of his or her instructional design options. In some cases, a service learning project may need to be a team effort

---

Title of Lesson

I. Problem Being Addressed Through the Service Learning Project and Anticipated Length of the Project

II. Anticipated Outcomes
  A. Behavioral
  B. Problem solving
  C. Expressive (to be generated by students at the end of the project)

III. Lessons Before the Service Learning Project
  A. Research/inquiry lesson(s)
  B. Data analysis lesson(s)
  C. Project planning lesson(s)

IV. Lessons Related to the Service Learning Project
  A. Lesson(s) conducted on site
  B. Lesson(s) conducted in the classroom

V. Lessons After the Service Learning Project
  A. Data interpretation lesson(s)
  B. Reflection and analysis of service learning experience lesson(s)

VI. Resources/Materials Needed to Conduct the Service Learning Project

---

FIGURE 8.4 Unit and Lesson Outline for a Service Learning Project

involving teachers from various content areas representing different teaching styles. Similarly, not every student will respond enthusiastically to a service learning project, especially if the experience comes later in the student's educational career. This suggests that some small-scale service-learning projects should be introduced in the early and middle childhood classrooms to provide a foundation for longer, more elaborate projects in junior high or high school if a school district wants to build service learning into its curriculum. Essential to the success of this planning model is a well-articulated, clearly conceived instructional design at each stage of planning.

Project- and Problem-Based Lesson Plans

Project-based and problem-based lesson plans share similar structural characteristics although the purposes differ somewhat. Project-based lessons tend to result in a product while problem-based lessons tend to be process oriented. Although a problem-based lesson may involve students in creating a product that solves a problem, the focus is primarily on problem solving and the successful product is a collateral benefit.

Both project-based and problem-based lessons can involve individual efforts or group efforts. Both require well-defined tasks with clear-cut roles for each person within a group. Individual problem-based learning (PBL) and project-based activities require a significant role for the student in determining the importance of the problem or the project in meeting his or her needs. The problems and the projects can address either social issues or personal issues relevant to that individual's life in the context of childhood, adolescence, and young adulthood. Examples of social issues would include such topics as terrorism, global warming, and the cost of medical care. Personal issues would include such topics as peer

I. Identify Context for the Problem
II. Process Objectives
III. Identify the Problem
IV. Define the Problem (students, individually or in teams, determine how to gather evidence)
V. Gather Facts (student[s] determine how to gather facts)
VI. Generate Questions (student[s] determine what needs to be known)
VII. Hypothesize (student[s] use scientific method to identify possible solutions)
VIII. Generate Alternatives (student[s] identify possible solution[s] to the problem)
IX. Lesson Closure (student[s] present solution[s] to the problem)
X. Assessment Strategies (effectiveness of the solution[s] and the process used is assessed)

FIGURE 8.5 Problem-Based Lesson Plan Model

Source: Kannel (2002).

I. Lesson Overview (describe project students will create, design, make, and so on)
II. Lesson Objectives (identify skills and abilities students will acquire through this project)
III. Preparation (introduce project, identify concepts/skills to be learned, discuss relevance of project to students and why it is meaningful to them, outline tasks to be accomplished)
IV. Practice and Process (gather preliminary information, do background research for the project, conduct activities that increase students' understanding of the project)
V. Performance (show end product of the project, submit project for review and modification, present project to class, school, community, and so on)
VI. Assessment (evaluate each step of the project to determine effectiveness of the process, evaluate the product that resulted from the project, create and use rubrics to evaluate process and product)

FIGURE 8.6 Project-Based Lesson Plan Model

Source: Edwards (2002).

pressure, bullying, and gender stereotyping. Crucial to both PBL and project-based learning activities, whether group or individual, is *authenticity*. If students don't perceive the problems and projects as authentic to them and their lives, both interest and motivation to complete the learning tasks will be minimal.

The sample lesson plan models for problem-based and project-based lessons include but vary somewhat from the elements of the basic lesson plan model in Figure 8.2. Although objectives may be stated before defining the problem or describing the project, these would primarily be process-oriented outcomes related to what the teacher expects students to learn as a result of engaging in problem solving or project design and development. What the students *actually* learn as a consequence of engaging in the process would more likely be stated as "expressive outcomes" (Eisner, 1979) as described in Chapters 4 and 6. This is because specific outcomes are difficult to predict when dealing with problem-based or project-based learning. Figures 8.5 and 8.6 illustrate how each of these types of lessons can be structured.

Problem-based and project-based lessons are powerful approaches to contextual teaching and learning. Most of these types of lessons run several days and involve considerable advance planning and an ability to modify each phase of the lesson spontaneously. Needless to say, they also require a high tolerance for ambiguity on the part of the teacher and the students! Although the lessons have a clear structure, there is also considerable fluidity in the daily activities as they unfold and evolve.

COOPERATIVE LEARNING:
THE JIGSAW MODEL

One of the learning environments used extensively in contextual teaching and learning is cooperative learning. This stems from the goal of creating classroom contexts in which cooperation among individuals and groups is emphasized over competition. Arguably, the best way for students to learn to cooperate is by experiencing a cooperative learning environment. Chapter 10 will discuss this more as it explores the design of classroom learning environments.

Although a number of planning models are categorized under the heading of cooperative learning, among the most popular is the Jigsaw Model, developed by Elliot Aronson (Gunter, Estes, & Schwab, 2003, p. 259). The Jigsaw Model places students into a context where they must work interdependently, rather than independently, to complete the learning task. Each student's work, individually and collectively, is "pieced together" to complete the task as though they were completing a jigsaw puzzle (Gunter et al., p. 259).

In the Jigsaw Model, students read information on a particular topic with other group members. The members discuss the topic in as much detail as possible, gathering additional information if necessary, until each member attains a satisfactory level of expertise. Other groups in the class are also studying a particular topic; all the topics are different but relate to a larger, more general topic. After each group studying a particular topic is finished, groups are reassembled with one member of each particular group assigned to a new group consisting of members drawn from all the other groups. Each member then shares his or her particular area of expertise with the other members until they collectively understand the larger, more general topic. In this way, each student learns about the larger, more general topic but only has to research his or her particular area in depth. The assumption is that by researching, discussing, and then teaching a topic, the student acquires a deeper understanding of a specialized topical area and a general understanding of a broader topic by viewing it from multiple perspectives (Gunter et al., pp. 259–264).

For example, if the more general topic were the U.S. government's impingement on individual rights and privileges, the specialized groups could first examine

I. Identify objectives for the lesson.
II. Introduce the Jigsaw topic, problem, or issue.
III. Assign students heterogeneously to their specialized study team to gather information and discuss their subtopic.
IV. Assemble "expert" groups with representatives from each of the specialized study teams with one member of each study team assigned to each expert group.
V. Have experts teach the members of their expert group about the specialized topic from their study group.
VI. Draw conclusions from each group and evaluate the process and the results.

FIGURE 8.7 The Jigsaw Model of Lesson Planning

Source: Gunter et al. (2003), pp. 259–264.

more specialized topics, such as gun control and the Second Amendment, maintaining a national database of DNA samples to solve crimes and the need to keep medical records private, and informing neighborhoods when a person convicted of a sex crime has moved into the area and that person's right to live wherever he or she wants to. Each group would study and debate its specialized topic until each member felt comfortable representing the group's informed perspective on its area of expertise. As the groups are reassembled with a member representing each of the specialized topics, the members share their particular area of expertise with this group. Ultimately, each of the reassembled groups reaches a collective conclusion regarding individual rights and the U.S. government's role in protecting the rights of all citizens. Although groups may reach different conclusions on this topic, they will all experience the need for interdependence when addressing complex problems and understand the importance of examining these problems from multiple perspectives.

Figure 8.7 outlines steps in the Jigsaw Model. The Jigsaw Model, along with the other alternative lesson planning models discussed in this chapter, contains common elements of the basic lesson planning model (Figure 8.3) but also contains unique elements. Although virtually every teacher can adapt the basic model to his or her teaching style, the alternative models may prove to be a more comfortable fit for some teachers than for others. All the models incorporate both behaviorist and constructivist theories of teaching and learning, and they all represent valid approaches to contextual teaching and learning, but not all models work in all learning environments for all kinds of teaching and learning styles. The next two chapters will explore strategies for helping teachers decide which modes work best for them.

Chapter 9 will examine how teachers can analyze the stages of instructional design involved in lesson planning and determine the extent to which their planning model represents effective teaching from a behaviorist and a constructivist perspective.

Finally, Chapter 10 will provide the instructional designer/classroom teacher with a holistic perspective on creating learning environments in the classroom through the use of research-based models of teaching (Joyce, Weil, & Calhoun, 2004).

REFERENCES

Ayers, W. (1993). *To teach: The journey of a teacher.* New York: Teachers College Press.

Bandura, A. (1977). *Social learning theory.* Englewood Cliffs, NJ: Prentice Hall.

Britzman, D. (1991). *Practice makes practice: A critical study of learning to teach.* Albany, NY: State University of New York Press.

Brophy, J., & Good, T. (1973). *Looking in classrooms.* New York: Harper & Row.

Bullough, R., & Gitlin, A. (1995). *Becoming a student of teaching: Methodologies for exploring self and school context.* New York: Garland.

Bybee, R. W. (Ed.). (1966). *National standards and the science curriculum Challenges, opportunities, and recommendations.* Dubuque, IA: Kendall-Hunt Publishers.

Clandinin, D. J. (1986). *Classroom practice: Teacher images in action.* Philadelphia: Falmer Press.

Connelly, M. (1988). *Teachers as curriculum planners: Narratives of experience.* New York: Teachers College Press.

Cruickshank, D. R., Jenkins, D. B., & Metcalf, K. K. (2003). *The act of teaching* (3rd ed.). Boston: McGraw-Hill.

Disney Learning Partnership. (2002). What is constructivism? Retrieved September 16, 2002, from http://www.thirteen.org/edonline/concept2class/month2/index_sub1.html

Edwards, G. (2002). Mountain Plains Distance Learning Partnership. Make your own project-based lesson plan. Retrieved September 16, 2002 from http://www.integrate learning.org

Eisner, E. (1979). The educational imagination. New York: Macmillan.

Evertson, C., & Emmer, E. T. (1982). Preventive classroom management. In D. Duke (Ed.), *Helping teachers manage classrooms.* Alexandria, VA: Association for Supervision and Curriculum Development.

Fever, M., & Towne, L. (2003). The logic and the basic principles of scientifically-based research. Retrieved December 15, 2003, from http://www.ed.gov/nclb/methods/whatworks/research/index.html

Gunter, M. A., Estes, T., & Schwab, J. (2003). Cooperative learning models: Improving student achievement using small groups. *Instruction: A models approach* (4th ed., pp. 256–264). Boston: Pearson.

Howey, K. (Ed.) (1998). *Contextual teaching and learning: Preparing teachers to enhance student success in and beyond school.* Columbus, OH: ERIC Clearinghouse on Adult, Career and Vocational Education.

Joyce, B., Weil, M., & Calhoun, E. (2004). *Models of teaching* (7th ed.). Boston: Pearson.

Kannel, J. (2002). PBL sample lesson plan. Retrieved November 20, 2003, from http://www.cesa10.k12.wi.US/clustera/summer/2002/Kannel/PBLLesson.htm

Posner, G., & Strike, K. (1976). A categorization scheme for principles of sequencing content. *Review of Educational Research, 46,* 665–690.

Rosenshine, B., & Furst, N. (1973). The use of direct observation to study teaching. In R. M. Travers (Ed.), *Second handbook of research on teaching.* Chicago. Rand McNally.

Zahorik, J. (1972). Teachers' planning models. *Educational Leadership, 33*(2), 134–139.

"5 Es instructional model." (2003). Retrieved November 20, 2003, from http://voyages through time.org/curriculum/instructional.html

"5 Es lesson components." (2003). Retrieved November 20, 2003, from http://mvhs1.mbhs.edu/mvhsproj/learningcycle/lcmodel.html

9

∾

Connecting Instructional Planning with Student Learning

U p to this point, the discussion on instructional design has focused on
structural and procedural issues related to the format for creating lesson
and unit plans. But format alone will not ensure successful instructional
design as measured by the achievement of student learning outcomes. Each day,
teachers make decisions that affect student learning, and, as might be expected,
many of these decisions occur during the planning process.

Researchers estimate that teachers make nearly a thousand decisions per day,
ranging from choosing what to teach to determining which student to call on to
answer a question (Chiarelott, Davidman, & Ryan, 1998). Of those myriad decisions, the ones related to what to teach and how to teach it will have the greatest
impact on student learning throughout all phases of teaching: planning, executing instruction, and assessment. However, making decisions is only part of the
process. Effective instructional design and, hence, effective teaching also depend
on the teacher's reflective analysis of those decisions.

The connection between reflective teaching and effective teaching has
been well established by researchers (Schoen, 1987) and teacher educators
(Cruickshank et al., 2003). For instructional designers, the connection will
occur at two key points: analyzing the stages of instructional design and assessing the instructional sequences created and used throughout the lesson. At both
points, designers must make connections between theories of learning, behavioral and constructivist, and research on effective teaching. Figures 9.1 and 9.2
illustrate the major components that must be reflectively analyzed at these two
key points.

I. Preassessment of students' existing knowledge or skill level
II. Identification of student learning outcomes
III. Creation of instructional sequences
IV. Postassessment based on determining students' attainment of learning outcomes

FIGURE 9.1 Stages of Instructional Design

I. Gaining student attention
II. Informing learner of the learning outcome(s)
III. Linking what is to be learned with previously learned concepts and skills
IV. Presenting material to be learned:
  A. Identifying concept/skill and providing examples (deductive)
  B. Presenting examples and having students draw conclusions (inductive)
V. Providing opportunity for students to use the concept or skill (guided practice)
VI. Supplying feedback on level of performance (formative)
VII. Assessing overall performance (summative)
VIII. Enhancing retention and transfer

FIGURE 9.2 Instructional Sequencing

Source: Adapted from Gagné and Briggs (1979).

Of the four stages of instructional design, the creation of instructional sequences will require ongoing analysis to determine if the student learning activities and teaching techniques selected are measurably increasing student learning. Figure 9.2 summarizes the eight components of instructional sequencing.

ANALYZING STAGES
OF INSTRUCTIONAL DESIGN

Although creating instructional sequences will be discussed in more depth later in the chapter, the other three stages of instructional design also require greater elaboration because they provide much of the foundational support for the instructional sequences. In most cases, the analysis of the three stages (pre- and postassessment and identification of student learning outcomes) will occur when the instructional unit is being constructed. However, the results of this analysis will also affect daily lesson planning and vice versa, so unit outcomes and assessments will have a continuing impact on a teacher's instructional decisions. Similarly, the teacher's decisions on a day-to-day basis will affect both outcomes and assessments.

Importance of Pre- and Postassessment

The importance of pre- and postassessment and their relationship to the ongoing analysis of effective instructional design cannot be overemphasized. The terms *preassessment* and *postassessment* are used rather than the more familiar pre- and post-test or testing (Dick & Carey, 1996, p. 143) because the latter terms suggest formal, written, usually objective forms of measurement. As noted in Chapters 6 and 7, assessment implies formal and informal, objective and subjective, written and performance-based formats inclusively. More to the point, however, assessment also includes the *interpretation* of what is being measured.

Many types of assessment devices are available for both formative assessment (for example, daily observations of children's performance) and summative assessments (for example, teacher-made unit tests and yearly proficiency tests). These data should be used to inform the teacher and the student of ongoing progress toward the attainment of learning outcomes. In that regard, teachers are encouraged to use criterion-referenced (Dick & Carey, 1996, p. 143) rather than norm-referenced assessments because criterion-referenced assessments provide data on performance and progress toward established criteria on an individual basis, whereas norm-referenced data provide comparisons between individual performance and other students' performance on a particular test. Norm-referenced data appear to be valid when individual comparisons are made to a large group (for example, statewide or districtwide proficiency test scores). Most classrooms of 25 or 30 students lack the large number of participants and the diversity of variables upon which the data can be normed. The average classroom doesn't provide anything close to a normal curve upon which students' performance scores could be plotted.

This means the instructional designer/classroom teacher will construct most pre- and postassessments. However, this discussion on pre- and postassessment will not describe various methods for constructing teacher-made tests. The focus here is on the purpose of assessing student performance in a CTL classroom.

Preassessment for CTL instructional design purposes generally occurs for two reasons: to assess students' prerequisite experiences and to assess students' entry-level knowledge of the concepts or skills to be learned. Before finalizing unit-level and even lesson-level objectives, the teacher needs to determine if the students have the prerequisite concepts, skills, and developmental maturity to attain the objectives successfully and/or if they have already attained a portion or all of the objectives previously.

Nearly every experienced teacher has had students, at one time or another, express dismay at the beginning of a lesson or a unit by protesting that they've already "done that" in another class or for a previous teacher. Although this may be true, it is essential for the teacher to determine that students have not only "done that," but also have actually *learned* and *retained* it. Such preassessment enables teachers to decide whether to teach an entire two-week unit or to only review major concepts and skills for one or two lessons and connect those concepts and skills to the next unit.

Another major purpose for preassessment in CTL is to determine which learning contexts will be most meaningful for the students. To do this, the students' prior experiences must be assessed so that relevant learning activities can be constructed. These data can be useful to teachers when deciding how to introduce a novel such as *Call of the Wild* to seventh graders as both an exciting adventure story and an engaging story about a transcendent relationship between a man and a dog and the challenges they face together. For some students, the promise of reading about adventure, competition, and even the challenges of nature might be interesting enough, but for others, reading about how a relationship between animals and humans can grow and become as powerful as any relationship between humans provides a much more meaningful learning experience. Teachers who are conscious of their students' prior experiences will be in a much better position to incorporate those experiences into the classroom.

So, if the purpose of preassessment is to determine students' pre-existing knowledge and experience prior to instruction, what is the purpose of postassessment? For instructional design purposes, postassessments provide data that indicate the extent to which students reached unit and lesson objectives and how much of that attainment can be attributed to instruction. In other words, did the learning experiences and activities selected by the instructional designer/teacher contribute to student achievement in a significant way or did classroom instruction make little or no impact on student learning? In a CTL classroom, this implies that if student achievement falls short of expectations, the fault is not in the students, presuming they *tried* to learn, but in the context in which learning was to have occurred.

Postassessments can take many forms, including objective measures of information retained to performance measures of how well that information was applied and transferred to an out-of-school context. Again, many resources are available for assisting teachers in designing appropriate assessment devices, but in selecting or creating these devices, the paramount concern should be for providing data about how students, individually and collectively, successfully attained the unit's or lesson's learning outcomes. This suggests that postassessments should be selected or created before or concurrent with unit and lesson design to reflect what is being *taught* along with what students are being expected to *learn*. Thus, waiting until the end of a five- or six-week unit to select or create a postassessment would not be a particularly wise decision for an instructional designer; the time lag between the lessons at the beginning of the unit and those at the end could impact which lessons postassessment emphasizes.

As a final cautionary note on postassessments, more frequent assessments are generally more useful and valid than long-term assessments. This suggests that end-of-semester cumulative final examinations probably provide a weaker database for determining student performance in a CTL classroom than do frequent, ongoing assessments. In this sense, assessments in a CTL classroom should be incremental rather than cumulative and be designed for continuous corrective feedback rather than for determining a grade at the end of a 12- to 18-week term.

Identifying Student Learning Outcomes

Student learning outcomes at both the unit and lesson level should clearly articulate what students will *learn* as a result of instruction. Since the early 1960s, the emphasis on performance or behavioral objectives has tended to focus on what students should be able to *do* as a result of instruction (Dick & Carey, 1996, p. 118) rather than what they will learn. Although the intent was to have teachers communicate specific behaviors that students would demonstrate following instruction, the emphasis on doing tended to result in statements of activities instead of outcomes. Elliot Eisner (1979, 1985) has persuasively argued for a broader definition of learning that builds upon and expands a substantial amount of student learning beyond behavioral performance to more complex discursive and nondiscursive types of outcomes, including problem solving and expressive outcomes. Chapters 6 and 7 discussed these types of outcome.

Because the format for writing student learning outcomes within and across domains and models has been discussed previously, this discussion will examine *why* these outcomes are so crucial for instructional design at the unit and lesson level. The major purpose for writing student learning outcomes is to provide a sense of direction for both the teacher and the student(s). If one views learning, metaphorically, as a journey, then outcome statements describe the idealized end of that journey. To paraphrase Lewis Carroll, it's difficult to know where you've been if you don't know where you're going! Outcome statements tell the learners where they are going, and more importantly, how they know when they've reached it. Whether the outcomes are behavioral, problem solving or expressive, cognitive, affective or psychomotor, they should guide the learners as they encounter new concepts, skills, beliefs, and values.

For example, if a physical education teacher tells students that they are expected to shoot successfully 5 of 10 free-throw shots an hour after instruction, then they could focus on the specific elements of shooting free throws accurately and practice part skills and the total skill until their performance was assessed. Although they may not be totally successful at the first performance assessment, they would know both the purpose and the outcome of instruction and then choose the appropriate response.

Not all "journeys" are that specific or unidirectional, however. In a junior high school science class, students might be given the objective of creating a container that will allow a raw egg to be dropped from a height of 30 feet to a concrete sidewalk and remain unbroken. The type of container, size, and composition of the padding inside the container could all be left to the students' discretion, but the learning outcome would remain the same for all students. With this problem-solving outcome, the context would determine the degree of success while each student or team of students would decide how to respond appropriately to that context. In this case, there would be several appropriate ways to complete the journey successfully.

In a sense, student learning outcomes create a circular structure for instructional design. At the unit level, unit outcomes provide guidance for the construction of lessons within the unit as well as for the pre- and postassessments that will determine the extent to which students have reached outcomes. At the lesson level, lesson outcomes identify both the starting and ending point for selecting and creating learning activities. Presumably, the lesson outcome indicates what students should be able to know, do, and/or feel as a result of instruction. The teacher can confidently state this because the preassessment should have established the students' entry-level knowledge, skills, and/or beliefs prior to instruction. Therefore, the journey has a logical beginning and a logical ending, and the teacher's role is to ensure that each student completes the journey successfully at some point as determined by the postassessment. *When* students reach the outcome(s) may vary widely depending on individual differences among learners, but if the outcomes are important, then the instructional design should provide the opportunity for all students to reach them successfully.

This suggests that student learning outcomes should represent the most crucial concepts, skills, attitudes, and values in a content area. A typical six-week unit should have no more than 25 or 30 unit-level outcomes, and a typical lesson should have only one or two objectives for a traditional 30- to 45-minute time frame. As is the case with concept overload in curriculum design, there is a tendency for outcome overload in instructional design. Selecting the one or two most important outcomes related to a concept, skill, attitude, or value will provide much more focus to the lesson design than will a lesson that tries to accomplish too much in too short a time frame.

INSTRUCTIONAL SEQUENCING

If the student learning outcomes provide the beginning and ending points of instruction, the sequencing of the lesson creates the circumference of the circle that connects the beginning and end. The basic lesson plan depicted in Figure 8.2 indicates that there is a logical progression in lesson design, suggesting that every lesson has a clear beginning, middle, and end.

The first three components (gaining student attention, informing the learner of the outcome, and linking what is to be learned with previously learned concepts and skills) make up the introductory phase of the lesson plan. Providing examples to illustrate a concept (deductive) or presenting examples to assist students in reaching a conclusion (inductive) represents the concept formation activities in the developmental phase of the lesson. Concepts and skills are then created and attained by providing guided practice and feedback on the students' level of performance to complete the developmental phase of the lesson. Finally, the concluding phase of the lesson involves the summative assessment of overall performance using the student learning outcomes as the criteria for assessment. Once overall performance is assessed, the circle is completed through the use of activities that enhance retention and transfer by applying concepts and skills within a new or different context.

THE INTRODUCTORY
PHASE OF THE LESSON

Gaining students' attention, informing the learner of the lesson outcomes, and linking what is to be learned with previously learned concepts or skills is generally referred to as "set induction" or "anticipatory set" (Hunter, 1985). The purpose of inducing a mental set is to prepare students adequately for learning. Using preassessment data, the teacher can construct an activity that connects the new concept or skill to be learned with concepts and skills learned in prior lessons or units as well as to previous experience. The teacher may also choose to create a shared experience—a video, field site visit, or guest speaker, for example—so all learners have a common experience related to the concept or skill that can be built upon in subsequent activities. This provides a context for student learning by establishing linkages between current learning outcomes and prior knowledge.

Research also suggests that informing students of the learning outcome can increase student achievement. Although studies show mixed results, ranging from no significant difference to significant differences, informing students of the learning outcome should generally produce a slight significant difference in increasing student achievement (Dick & Carey, 1996, p. 118). Indeed, common sense suggests that learners would perform better if they knew ahead of time what the expectations were, but this could vary somewhat depending on the individual learner and the learning environment that the teacher creates. Suffice to say that it probably isn't going to hurt achievement any by informing the students of the learning outcome.

However, neither linking current concepts and skills to prior knowledge nor informing students of the learning outcome is likely to be successful if the teacher hasn't gained that student's attention. Researchers (Brophy & Good, 1983; Evertson, 1979; Hunter, 1985) long ago established the difference between a successful lesson and an unsuccessful lesson as resting largely on the teacher's ability to begin the lesson with all students completely engaged in learning. Although the time a student spends on a learning task is important, that time is wasted if a student isn't fully engaged in the task. Educators and parents frequently decry children's short attention span, but one has only to observe children at the computer on the Internet or playing a video game to see that attention span isn't the problem. What children have is a low tolerance for boredom brought on by the "media-ated" culture and the wealth of information and experience available outside the classroom (Chiarelott, 1983). Although teachers will never be able to compete with the stimuli outside the classroom, this context must be acknowledged and brought into the classroom to connect with learners' experiences (Chiarelott, 1983).

There will be times when the content being presented is so inherently interesting and engaging to the student that a powerful set induction activity will be unnecessary. However, when the content is new to the learner or is highly complex and difficult to learn or has no obvious discernible interest to the student, then some kind of set induction activity must be part of the lesson's introductory phase. Essentially, the intention is to create an activity wherein the student identifies a need to learn that particular concept or skill.

Outside of the field of education, for example, advertisers are acutely aware of the importance of creating a link between the product and the consumer. In a wide variety of ways, advertisers appeal to the consumer's need for acceptance, popularity, good health, and status by suggesting that their product will meet that need. This is especially true when the product is geared toward something an individual would not choose to do if he or she had a choice. One only has to visit a few garage sales to find little used exercycles, treadmills, and NordicTracks® to determine that advertising can induce people to purchase something that they didn't realize they actually needed. Unfortunately, the connection was only to the need and not to how to apply that product to meet that need.

This example points up an important issue for teachers when designing set induction activities. A powerful set induction activity does not necessarily result in meaningful learning. First, the attention-getting activity has to be clearly connected to the concept or skill to be learned. Second, the set induction activity can't be so powerful that the rest of the lesson pales in comparison. This would be similar to an advertisement that shows all the funniest or most exciting scenes in a new movie in the preview. Unfortunately, the movie itself turns out to be a disappointment, and ticket sales drop dramatically when the word gets out about the film itself. Third, if a need is identified in the set induction activity, then it must be met in the lesson itself. If the set induction activity promises that students will see how learning about polynomial equations will help them perform a job more successfully, then the rest of the lesson has to deliver on that promise. Otherwise, all the set induction activity has done is to create a need without meeting it. This, of course, points out the importance of linking the introductory phase of the lesson to the developmental and concluding phases.

The Developmental Phase of the Lesson

The developmental phase of the lesson is so named because its activities help students develop and attain the concept or skill. In a contextual teaching and learning classroom, these activities would contain examples derived from real situations, events, and problems. Students would be encouraged to analyze and apply these examples deductively (working from a general conclusion or solution supported by evidence drawn from examples) and/or inductively (working from specific examples and drawing a generalizable conclusion or solution).

For example, before visiting an art museum to study Impressionistic artists, students would receive background information on attributes of Impressionistic art in the classroom. Examples derived from the works of Van Gogh, Monet, Degas, Seurat, and others would be analyzed in class to identify both the criterial and noncriterial attributes of some of their paintings. These findings would then be applied to their visit to the art museum. This deductive approach would enable the students to gather evidence to support the definition of Impressionism given to them in class before applying that definition in the context of the museum visit.

The same activity could also be done inductively. Rather than starting with a definition and examples to support that definition, students would locate examples of art works by Van Gogh, Monet, Degas, Seurat, and other painters and then analyze them to identify what they perceive to be the common criterial attributes shared among those art works. Working from those criterial attributes and an emerging definition of Impressionism, students would analyze a new set of examples along with some nonexamples. This would enable students to verify their findings as well as to identify noncriterial attributes in both examples and nonexamples. As in the deductive activity, the students would culminate their investigation with a trip to the art museum to test their findings and apply the concepts they had just learned.

As a general rule, a lesson designed to use inductive or deductive thinking should use a sufficient number of examples to illustrate the concept. Researchers suggest using five to seven different examples when teaching a concept that is new or difficult for the students to learn (Martorella, 1990, pp. 150–184). If nonexamples are used, they should be introduced after the positive examples are thoroughly analyzed and understood so that students don't confuse examples and nonexamples. Such confusion can lead to the formation of misconceptions.

Key to the successful development and attainment of concepts and skills is the opportunity to have guided practice with timely corrective feedback. Guided practice and corrective feedback are important decision points in the instructional sequencing process, but they are frequently overlooked or handled inappropriately. In most cases, the major problem is the teacher not allocating sufficient time in class for guided practice with corrective feedback from the teacher. In fact, one of the major arguments for block scheduling and teaming in the junior high and high school is that these structures provide more time for practicing a concept or skill under the guidance of one or more teachers.

This leads to a topic of considerable concern in the area of guided practice with timely corrective feedback. That topic is *homework*. Numerous studies have researched the benefits and problems associated with homework, and Harris Cooper summarizes them effectively in his book *Homework* (Cooper, 1989). Many educators and parents argue that homework teaches students responsibility, time management skills, goal-setting strategies, and study skills, and these arguments are generally indisputable. However, homework also needs to be done under the proper conditions and at an appropriate point in the learning process, or the result is likely to be frustration, anger, procrastination, cheating, and the development of misconceptions (Cooper, 1989, pp. 17–28).

Homework, either compulsory or voluntary, can assist student learning if it allows students to apply concepts or skills that have been attained through the guidance of and feedback from the teacher. However, homework should not be assigned because the material wasn't covered in class. Similarly, parents should not be expected to provide the environment for guided practice and feedback of material that was not covered sufficiently in class either. The potential for the formation of poor study skills and misconceptions should be obvious.

Problems also occur when students receive a few examples in class and then are asked to complete an assignment at home that includes those examples along with different, new, or more complex examples. In that context, students will have one of three outcomes: they successfully teach themselves the new, different, or more complex concepts or skills; they try to learn the new material but teach themselves incorrectly, thus forming a misconception that would need to be "unlearned" later; or they reach a frustration level with the new material and just quit working. In the latter two scenarios, the homework assignment has actually created more problems for the learner and the teacher.

Homework is sometimes assigned to prepare students for the next day's lesson and this, at least in theory, seems to be a good idea. If this homework strategy is used, however, the teacher does need to consider some potential consequences that will affect the design of the lesson plan for the next class. For example, if students are assigned to read a short story at home to prepare for an in-class discussion the next day, what will the teacher do if no one reads the story? If only half the class reads the story? Or, if problems are assigned in a math class so that students can discuss the solution to those problems in the next class, what happens if students only do some of the problems? If the students do the problems but do them incorrectly? Although both situations are potentially salvageable, they also create challenges for the teacher that are of his or her own doing. The purpose of homework should not be to create more problems for teachers and students, but ill-conceived or inappropriately timed assignments can do just that.

So, what kind of homework is valuable while not creating more difficulties for the teacher? First, homework should be a logical extension of the instruction and assessment the teacher provides in class. Second, the homework should allow students to work independently successfully. This means that sufficient practice and corrective feedback have already been supplied in class so that the chances for successful completion of the homework are high for all students. Third, if the assignment is designed to prepare students for the next day's class, the lesson should not be predicated on all students doing the assignment correctly and completely. For example, a reasonable homework assignment to prepare students for a discussion on plants and animals would be to ask them to locate examples of plants and animals they can see around the school, at home, and in their neighborhood and to bring a list of five of those examples to school the next day. In this assignment, if only half of the students do it, there are still plenty of examples to use in the lesson. If a student doesn't do it, he or she can still learn from the discussion in class, and there is no reason to punish the student for not doing the assignment. Fourth, students should see the relevance of the assignment to what they've learned and to their own experiences. This would suggest that "busy work" or homework assigned just to be sure that students are doing homework every night is not a good practice. Fifth, the timing and length of homework assignments should be realistic and sensitive to the amount of homework assigned in other classes. It is a highly questionable practice to have students doing four to six hours of homework one night and none the next night because teachers did not time their assignments appropriately. Finally, if homework that requires corrective feedback from the teacher is assigned, the homework should be assessed in a timely fashion so that students receive feedback within 24 hours. There is nothing more frustrating to a student than to complete an assignment on time but not receive feedback from the teacher for a week or 10 days, or, in some extreme cases, never. Teachers need to determine what is realistic for them to correct and assess within 24 hours (or the next class) before assigning a task for homework.

This discussion on the benefits and challenges of homework establishes the need for meaningful closure in contextual teaching and learning. To assess performance effectively and to enhance retention and transfer, the guided practice and corrective feedback must be given in a context relevant to the students' experience and prior learning while also providing a bridge to subsequent learning. The importance of assessing performance and enhancing retention and transfer in context cannot be overemphasized.

The Concluding Phase of the Lesson

The purpose of the lesson's concluding phase to provide closure to the students. Although closure can take many forms, it is usually designed to enable the teacher to determine if students have reached the objectives for the lesson. There may be times when closure occurs serendipitously at a key point in a lesson because a student or the teacher provides a perfect example, asks an insightful question, or simply connects to the experiences of the learners in such a way that understanding is immediately observable among the students. In most cases, however, closure has to be carefully planned to include review, performance assessment, and an opportunity to ensure retention and transfer.

In a CTL classroom, closure should include an authentic assessment whereby students are able to apply the concept or skill in a context that is relevant to them. Robert Sternberg (2003) suggests that teachers help develop "expert students" by teaching practical knowledge that involves an application of what students know to an authentic situation. This is similar to the purpose of closure in a CTL classroom in which the teacher uses authentic situations to assess performance. This performance is then transferred to a new or unfamiliar context, thereby reinforcing the need for the concept or skill and enhancing the potential for retaining the concept or skill beyond the end of the lesson.

If closure is not provided at transition points in a lesson, students will tend to supply their own form of closure. This is because most humans feel the need to achieve closure at various points of their daily experiences. Whether it involves punching a time clock at the end of a workday to having an episode of their favorite TV show end happily, to terminating a relationship symbolically, people tend to want to know when an experience has ended so they can move on to their next experience. Not having a degree of closure can create a sufficient level of cognitive dissonance to make a person feel psychologically incomplete. If this occurs too frequently in a person's life, as well as in a classroom, feelings of confusion and frustration begin to arise.

In a CTL classroom, performance is assessed in contexts that are relevant to the learner and authentic to the area of performance being assessed. Although there will be opportunities for closure at transition points and at the end of a daily lesson, activities designed to assess performance and enhance transfer and retention will probably occur less frequently because they need to be embedded within an authentic context (for example, a service learning setting, laboratory setting, or field trip setting). This will require significantly more planning to locate settings that are appropriate to the concepts and skills being taught and to the experiential base of the students. Thus, in a CTL classroom, closure can be used in an ongoing, daily, formative micro context in the classroom and in a periodic, cumulative, summative macro context within sites inside and outside the classroom.

As this discussion of the stages of instructional design and the phases of instructional sequencing indicates, teachers must make decisions constantly, as in any classroom. However, in a CTL classroom, these decisions must be linked to appropriate theories of teaching and learning in a manner consistent with the CTL philosophy. Further, teachers must approach these decisions in a reflective, analytic manner to ensure that student learning involves an experience-based, authentic approach to both planning and executing instruction.

Although this decision-making process may appear to be incremental and segmented, it actually should be holistic and integrated in a CTL classroom. To foster this approach to planning instruction, CTL teachers are encouraged to think of instructional planning as the construction of learning environments. To facilitate this process, models of teaching that are appropriate to CTL need to be identified. In Chapter 10, a group of models are analyzed and applied to the CTL classroom to furnish the kind of holistic, integrative approach to instructional planning needed in a successful CTL classroom.

REFERENCES

Brophy, J., & Good, T. (1973) *Looking in classrooms.* New York: Harper & Row.

Chiarelott, L., Davidman, L., & Ryan, K. (1998). *Lenses on teaching.* Belmont, CA: Wadsworth.

Cooper, H. (1989). *Homework.* New York: Longman.

Cruickshank, D. R., Jenkins, D. B., & Metcalf, K. K. (2003). *The act of teaching* (3rd ed.). Boston: McGraw-Hill.

Dick, W., & Carey, L. (1996). *The systematic design of instruction* (4th ed.). Summit, NJ: HarperCollins.

Eisner, E. (1979). *The educational imagination.* New York: Macmillan.

Hunter, M. (1985). *Mastery teaching.* El Segundo, CA: TIP Publications.

Schoen, D. (1987). *Educating the reflective practitioner: Toward a new design for teaching and learning in the professions.* San Francisco: Jossey-Bass.

Sternberg, R. (November 2003). What is an "expert" student? *Educational Researcher, 32*(8), 5–9.

10

Creating Learning Environments

Historically, a behaviorist philosophy has dominated instructional design literature and the discourse on effective teaching. As the literature on effective teaching has burgeoned over the past 30 to 35 years, other philosophies have begun to emerge that challenge the assumptions about teaching and learning promulgated by the "scientifically based" approaches supported by behaviorism. Most notably, curriculum theorists such as William Pinar, Bill Ayers, Deb Britzman, and Janet Millet began challenging these approaches as early as 1973, but particularly in the past 10 to 15 years. Another group of theorists led by Elliot Eisner and Thomas Barone articulated an aesthetically based approach to teaching that suggested that effective teaching was as much an art as it was a science. These theorists tend to support a constructivist perspective on teaching and learning.

Although these philosophical differences seem to suggest an "either/or" position on effective teaching, a more defensible position would involve locating these apparently competing positions on a continuum and arguing that effective teaching, in a CTL classroom anyway, involves aspects of both. As noted in Chapters 8 and 9, well-designed instruction should respond to the context in which the instruction will occur. In a CTL classroom, this means that sometimes a behaviorist approach best fits the context and other times a constructivist approach fits best.

Up to this point, instructional designs might appear to involve a series of discrete decisions made in a linear fashion as the designer selects appropriate content, outcomes, introductory, developmental, and concluding activities and finally assesses the results of instruction. However, that would not be consistent with the purpose of contextual teaching and learning. Effective instructional design in a CTL classroom requires the designer to create a *learning environment* by conceptualizing the classroom in a holistic fashion as an ecological system. This system must balance learner, societal, and content needs through the allocation and distribution of available resource such as time, space, instructional materials (including technology), and human resources (students, teachers, parents).

In a CTL classroom, the teacher must decide when the learning environment requires a behaviorist approach and when it requires a constructivist approach. Although a behaviorist philosophy would support such teaching models as *direct instruction* and a constructivist philosophy would support such teaching models as *inquiry based,* it would be simplistic to conclude that behaviorist models work best for lower-level, skill-oriented content and outcomes and constructivist models work best with higher-level, conceptually complex content and outcomes. It would be safer to conclude that behaviorist models work best when the content and outcomes require a predictable, definable performance, an observable, measurable behavior, and a teacher-controlled environment. This would include modeling desired behaviors, reinforcing appropriate responses, and repeating, through practice, acceptable performances.

Constructivist models work best when the content and outcomes allow for a range of possible acceptable responses, some of which may not be immediately discernible to the teacher when planning instruction. There may be several correct ways to reach the outcome(s), and there may be no *single* correct answer. Rather than having students repeat a performance correctly, the teacher is more concerned with what the performance means to the student or why the student chose to perform the activity in a certain way. In a constructivist model, the student could have more control over the learning environment than the teacher has, especially in a self-directed model or in a situation where a unique product, rather than a similar product, was required of students, such as in a Synectic Model (Joyce & Weil, 1972).

Other models could show evidence of both a behaviorist and a constructivist philosophy. An example of this would be the Group Investigation Model (Joyce, Weil, & Calhoun, 2004, pp. 219–227) in which the teacher might need to use a behaviorist approach to establish appropriate group behaviors in assigning tasks, interacting interpersonally, and using effective work habits. Once the group was established and functioning successfully, a constructivist approach would emerge that would encourage the group members to collect and interpret data, draw conclusions, and describe possible solutions to the problem; their ultimate task is to explain *why* the group members individually and collectively felt that they solved the problem correctly. This blended approach to creating a learning environment would represent an effective strategy for balancing both behaviorist and constructivist philosophies in the classroom.

How do behaviorism and constructivism approach different elements of a learning environment separately and in a blended format? Table 10.1 juxtaposes these three perspectives to demonstrate their areas of divergence and convergence.

In a contextual teaching and learning classroom, one would expect to see greater evidence of a blended philosophy rather than a purely behaviorist or constructivist philosophy, but this does not preclude the possibility that one could successfully use "pure" philosophy in a CTL classroom. The crucial point is that the teacher has

Table 10.1 Philosophical Perspectives on Learning Environments

	Behaviorism (DeMar, 1997)	Constructivist (Henriques, 2002)	Blended
Learning Environment	Teacher controlled; students respond to stimuli presented by the teacher; teacher designs the environment to maximize desired responses from the student.	Teacher mediates environment; students control own behavior; students construct meaning from experiences embedded in the learning environment.	Teacher structures an environment that maximizes opportunity for desired behaviors to be performed and meaning constructed from those experiences.
Student	Responds to environment; establishes pattern of behavior that demonstrates ability to form and develop concepts and skills as determined by an external "authority" (that is, the content the teacher provides); responds positively to rewards given by the teacher, the environment, or both.	Viewed as a "thinker" with emerging theories about the world; provides interpretive constructions of concepts and skills that the teacher builds on in subsequent lessons; students pose questions rather than responding to them; establishes internal reward system based on satisfaction derived from understanding and appreciating experiences.	Sees the importance of and need for correct responses and the need to ask good questions; uses information acquired from the content as a foundation to build upon in constructing meaning from experience; requires both external symbols of success and internal reward systems.
Teacher	Disseminates information and experience to students; selects and structures the curriculum and learning experiences; uses learning principles of reinforcement, repetition, and contiguity in a planned, systematic approach to instruction; expects student responses to be similar, although not always the same.	Guides and facilitates learning; creates an environment with few if any correct answers but expects students to challenge, deconstruct, and reconstruct the curriculum; uses interpretation and construction of meaning from experience as primary learning principle; designs basic lesson plan, but student voice plays an important role in determining the course of the lesson; expects unique, not identical, responses from learners.	Directs lessons to establish a conceptual, informational base, but transitions to a student-directed format when appropriate; works from established curriculum but connects students' experiences to the curriculum and vice versa; enables predictable and unique responses to performances; uses both behaviorist and constructivist theories of teaching and learning as appropriate to the context.
Assessment	Measurable and/or observable, usually involving a performance assessed against a standard benchmark or a paper and pencil response; teacher made or standardized and usually quantifiable; responses should be the same as or similar to the model provided; usually follows instruction.	Usually qualitative and may involve teacher observations of students at work, portfolios, or exhibitions; performance may be assessed by a rubric, but unique responses or interpretations must be incorporated; use of authentic assessments is encouraged; is usually embedded in instruction rather than following instruction; teacher determines *why* a certain response was made rather than just assessing the response.	Contextual and may involve the ability to demonstrate knowledge of important information as well as use and transfer concepts and skills to new contexts; uses both authentic and paper and pencil assessments; embedded in the context but may occur during or after instruction; teacher expects correct responses and also wants to know *why* students responded as they did.

thoroughly analyzed the context and has consciously decided that the philosophy chosen matches and is best for the context. This also assumes that the teacher is viewing the learning environment from a holistic perspective that incorporates a "theory in practice" as the learning environment is created.

The most effective way to view a learning environment holistically is to use the perspective embodied in *Models of Teaching* (1972) first conceptualized by Bruce Joyce and Marsha Weil and expanded upon by Joyce, Weil, and Calhoun (2004) as well as by Mary Alice Gunter, Thomas Estes, and Jan Schwab in *Instruction: A Models Approach* (2002). Using these resources, we will examine six different models—Concept Attainment, Inductive, Synectic, Group Investigation, Inquiry Training, and Self-Directed Learning—as they represent aspects of behavioristic, constructivist, or blended approaches to creating learning environments.

THE CONCEPT ATTAINMENT MODEL

Chapter 5 discussed concepts and how concepts are formed, developed, and attained. Concept mapping allows the curriculum designer to categorize a set of related concepts hierarchically in superordinate, coordinate, and subordinate relationships. The Concept Attainment Model builds on the discussion of concept attributes, criterial and noncriterial, as well as how to help students organize their conceptual schema as depicted through concept mapping.

The Concept Attainment Model is essentially an inductive approach to teaching concepts (Gunter, Estes, & Schwab, 2003, p. 81), but it is more teacher directed and behavioristic philosophically than the other models discussed in this chapter. The theoretical basis for the model is drawn from research conducted by Jerome Bruner, Jacqueline Goodnow, and George Austin (Gunter, Estes, & Schwab, 2003, p. 91) in the late 1950s. Their research suggested that the process of categorizing data assisted in attaining concepts (p. 92). According to Gunter et al., Bruner and his colleagues postulated three rules for concept attainment:

1. Take the first positive instance and make it into your initial hypothesis.
2. Consider what is common to your hypothesis and any positive-informing instances you may encounter.
3. Ignore everything else.

In other words, once an initial set of examples has identified the criterial attributes of a concept, students should examine additional examples and nonexamples to see if the initial hypothesis (or definition) of the concept holds up, and then ignore the noncriterial attributes that make up part of the concept but don't define it.

For example, if students are studying the concept of *mammal,* they would initially hypothesize (or define) the characteristics of a mammal. The teacher would then present positive examples of mammals and ask students to find the common characteristics of mammals based on their hypothesis. At this point, both criterial and noncriterial attributes would be identified by the students with the teacher's assistance. Once the teacher was confident that students understood the concept,

Phase One:	Teacher presents *numerous* examples. Students develop a hypothesis about how the examples fit or don't fit.
Phase Two:	Students analyze the strategy they need to *attain the concepts*.
Phase Three:	Teacher presents a new set of examples, some that illustrate the concept (positive examples) and others that don't (nonexamples). Students determine which examples fit.
Phase Four:	Students develop new categories for organizing and classifying the examples or develop alternative hypotheses or definitions.

FIGURE 10.1 The Concept Attainment Model

he or she would present examples and nonexamples and ask students again to identify the criterial attributes of mammals and ignore the noncriterial attributes because they would not define the concept. Further assessment would help test the initial hypothesis, redefine it if necessary, or, in some cases, create an alternative hypothesis (definition) or subhypotheses (additional definitions).

The critical point in instructional planning for the Concept Attainment Model is the selection of examples. At each step of the model requiring examples and nonexamples, as many as five to seven different examples and nonexamples may be needed to ensure that students have sufficient opportunity to analyze each example and practice applying the hypothesis (definition) to a new example(s). The assessment of whether the concept was attained should employ different examples and nonexamples in the same context or use the same (or similar) examples and nonexamples in a new context. Figure 10.1 summarizes the steps in the Concept Attainment Model.

THE INDUCTIVE MODEL

Hilda Taba, a pioneer in social studies education and a prominent curriculum theorist in the 1950s and 1960s, created the Inductive Model, also known as the Concept Development Model (Gunter, Estes, & Schwab, 2003, p. 97; Joyce, Weil, & Calhoun, 2004, pp. 41–58). Taba argued that inductive thinking was the way humans naturally formed concepts by working from specific examples and then drawing conclusions (part-to-whole thinking). This suggests that while children and adults may differ in *what* they think about, the process of *how* they think is similar from an inductive perspective (Gunter et al., p. 108).

The Inductive Model can include specific, defined outcomes and use a teacher-directed strategy to guide students through the inductive thinking process, so it does have philosophical roots in behaviorism. However, as the process unfolds, students begin to construct their own methods of using inductive thinking, so in that respect, the model also has philosophic roots in constructivism, especially because it consciously involves teaching a process of thinking. Although a lesson using the Inductive Model could be completed in a single, one-day lesson, in many cases the Inductive Model requires several (three to five) days' lessons, especially if the entire model is used.

Phase One:	Teacher has students suggest examples and list them.
Phase Two:	Examples are grouped according to similarities.
Phase Three:	Groupings are labeled.
Phase Four:	Students *identify* relationships among groupings.
Phase Five:	Students *explain* relationships among groupings.
Phase Six:	Students draw inferences to interpret the data they've generated.
Phase Seven:	Students generalize about the concept(s) and develop hypothesis(es) to test these generalizations.
Phase Eight:	Students present evidence to support the hypothesis(es).
Phase Nine:	Students test and verify their predictions.

FIGURE 10.2 The Inductive Model

For example, in a fifth-grade science class, a teacher may spend one day helping students categorize examples of living things they were asked to locate and list based on their observations at school, on the playground, in their neighborhood, and at home. These categories would then receive "working" labels based on the similar characteristics found among the examples in each categorical grouping. That entire activity would probably take one science class.

In the next class, students would be asked to identify how each group related to the other groups based upon the characteristics of the examples in each group. Primarily, the students would identify relationships between plants and animals but other kingdoms (up to five) could be added, depending on the examples provided and the developmental level of the students. The students would then explain the relationships and make inferences about how these relationships affect living things positively and negatively. This activity would probably require a second day's class time and lead to the final phases of the model, which could take another one to five days.

The final three phases of the Inductive Model would require students to generalize based on the inferences they've drawn and develop a hypothesis (or hypotheses) about how living things relate to one another. They would then research this hypothesis by gathering data, testing the data, and verifying their hypothesis as valid, invalid, or in need of modification. Ultimately, they could define and depict such phenomena as the life cycle, photosynthesis, and symbiotic and parasitic relationships. Through the teacher's guidance, the students would learn to think inductively, moving from specific example to verifiable generalizations.

Of course, not every concept or set of concepts can be presented using this model, nor would it be appropriate to use the Inductive Model to teach every class every day. The creation of a learning environment based in inductive thinking is a necessary but not sufficient approach to effective teaching. As in the Concept Attainment Model, a teacher would need to determine which approach to the development of thinking skills would work best given the content and the context. Figure 10.2 provides an overview of the Inductive Model for comparison purposes so that teachers can make an instructional decision appropriate to the content being taught and the context in which it will be learned.

THE GROUP INVESTIGATION MODEL

The Group Investigation Model provides the teacher with ample opportunities to incorporate effective teaching practices derived from both the behaviorist and the constructivist philosophies. This model is deeply rooted in the progressive philosophy of John Dewey and was first developed by one of his disciples, Herbert Thelen (Joyce, Weil, & Calhoun, 2004, pp. 219–227). Thelen argued that all knowledge was the result of a social construction, meaning that people negotiate what is known through interactions with others and construct reality based on those interactions. So, for example, what is "known" about the health risks of firsthand and secondhand smoking tends to be a blend of the findings by independent scientists, scientists working for tobacco companies, and public policy makers who must balance the needs of the tobacco industry and the needs of the consumer with the general welfare of society. Ultimately, the individual then decides what he or she "knows" and behaves accordingly.

These types of problems are central to how the Group Investigation Model functions. The problem must be genuine and the students must perceive it as a problem worth solving. The problem could be derived directly from the content being studied or it could be a problem that exists in a larger social context that allows students to integrate the concepts and skills from one or more content areas. The problem must also be sufficiently complex that it requires a group effort to reach a solution, and it must be structured so that each student in the group is responsible for a different task. Each task must constitute a component of the solution so that each student's work is interdependent with the other students' work. The parts (individual group members' tasks) all contribute to forming the whole (the solution to the problem). By working cooperatively, the students accomplish more than they could accomplish on their own.

This brings up an important element of group work. Use group work as a teaching strategy when the content and the context present a problem that can only be solved through an interdependent, cooperative group effort. Too often teachers are persuaded that they should do group work occasionally to be effective, creative teachers. Sometimes this merely involves putting students in groups to perform a task that any one of the students in the group could do himself or herself. Unfortunately, that's exactly what happens with some group projects as one or two task-oriented students take on all the responsibility for doing the group project because they don't want their grades to suffer as a result of the procrastination or laziness of the other group members. Rather than learning about the benefits of working in groups, these students learn that group work inhibits their learning because the group is actually slowing them down from what they could learn on their own.

From a behaviorist perspective, this suggests that students have to learn to behave appropriately in a cooperative learning group such as the type required in the Group Investigation Model. Before using the model, the teacher must take the time to demonstrate how groups should function during a group investigation. The appropriate behaviors should be modeled and reinforced positively when students perform them. The teacher should never assume that the students will be able to function successfully as group members no matter what the content area or grade level of the students.

Phase One:	Students confront a problem situation derived from the subject matter.
Phase Two:	Students share their reactions to and feelings about the problem situation.
Phase Three:	Students narrow down the situation into a specific problem to investigate.
Phase Four:	Students analyze the problem, devise tasks to undertake to reach its solution, and assign tasks to individual members.
Phase Five:	Students complete their tasks and report the findings.
Phase Six:	Students evaluate their solution(s) according to the original purposes of the group.

FIGURE 10.3 The Group Investigation Model

Once the teacher is satisfied that the students understand the Group Investigation Model and how group members should function successfully, the problem should be introduced to the students. The teacher should relate the problem to the content area(s) being investigated, and the students should share their reactions to the importance and relevance of the problem and its solution.

For example, if students are examining the effects of terrorism on society in general and their lives in particular, this topic would then be broken down into four or five subtopics that each group would investigate: for example, terrorism and religion, the politics of terrorism, the historical roots of terrorism in the United States, and terrorism as an international problem. Each group of five to seven students would either be assigned or would select a subtopic for that group to investigate. With four or five such groups, a class of 20 to 30 students could be using the Group Investigation Model for several days or even weeks. The group members would then break down the assigned or selected subtopics into individual tasks for each group member to address. For the group investigating terrorism as an international problem, each group member could examine terrorism in a different part of the world (the Middle East, Europe, Asia, North America). After each member collects and analyzes the information from his or her area, the group then collates this information and offers the findings to the entire class. Each of the other subtopic groups does the same thing, and then the entire class discusses all the findings and offers possible solutions. Finally, each group member, each subtopic group, and the entire class assess both the products and the process.

Figure 10.3 summarizes the phases of the Group Investigation Model as described in the preceding example. This model, more so than the previous two, requires the teacher's role to be that of a guide, facilitator, resource person, and taskmaster and thus would not be considered a teacher-directed model. This role is fairly typical of group work done under the general heading of cooperative learning and may not be fully comfortable for a teacher who prefers a more teacher-controlled learning environment. However, if done correctly, this model can provide considerable teacher control over how the groups function, but much less control over what the group members conclude on the basis of their investigation. In that sense, the Group Investigation Model provides a balance between the behaviorist and the constructivist philosophies.

THE INQUIRY MODEL

The use of inquiry or discovery learning as the basis for enabling students to teach themselves emerged from the national curriculum projects, particularly in the sciences of the late 1950s and 1960s. The scientists who guided these curriculum reform efforts argued that merely telling students about scientific concepts and principles was insufficient and ineffectual. Students needed to experience the process of inquiry and discovery as scientists did. Students spend most of their time in school answering questions posed by the teacher, but they rarely get the opportunity to *ask* questions that might help guide and structure their thinking. More importantly, teachers didn't teach students how to ask good questions or provide direct experiences in the classroom that would enable students to develop this skill.

In the early 1960s, Richard Suchman developed a model to train students on how to ask questions to guide inquiry (Gunter, Estes, & Schwab, 2003, p. 118; Joyce, Weil, & Calhoun, 2004, pp. 119–130). He felt that students entered school full of questions and naturally curious and that the process of traditional teaching and learning squelched these natural characteristics of children by late childhood or early adolescence. Thus, teachers needed a model that would help students rediscover their natural curiosity and propensity for questioning what they didn't understand. The Inquiry Training Model was developed to meet this need.

Although the Inquiry Training Model appears to fit best in the sciences, it has wide applicability across all content areas (Gunter et al., p. 119). The purpose of the model is to present students with a puzzling event, problem, or experimental demonstration for which there is no obvious, immediate answer, solution, or explanation. Ostensibly, the teacher knows the correct answer, solution, or explanation, but rather than simply telling the students (which they would promptly forget), the teacher guides them through a series of questions posed by various students until they appear to be able to offer a credible hypothesis. However, the questions the students pose must be stated in such a way that the teacher can only answer yes or no. The teacher may provide some additional guidance or information (p. 119), but the students must do the hypothesizing.

As each yes and no question is asked and responded to, the teacher or another student keeps track of the responses so that students can see which questions generated which response. They are also cautioned that a *no* may be as valuable or more valuable than a *yes* response because it helps eliminate false leads or faulty information. Finally, when enough data have been collected and analyzed through questions, students are encouraged to present possible answers, solutions, or explanations to the phenomenon they explored.

For example, a sixth-grade science teacher might begin the class by showing the students a peeled hard-boiled egg and a quart milk bottle and explaining that she has been puzzling over how to get the egg in the bottle without damaging the egg. She would then tell the students that she figured out a way to get the egg in the bottle, but she wanted to know why it worked. After lighting a small piece of paper on fire and dropping it into the bottom of the bottle, she placed the smaller end of the egg into the top of the bottle whereupon the egg suddenly

Phase One:	Through observation, the students learn as much as possible about the objects or events by asking questions and generating hypotheses, determine the conditions of the object(s) before and after the events occur, and organize the data they've generated to discover relationships.
Phase Two:	Through analysis, the students separate the useful data from other useless or unrelated data.
Phase Three:	Through reflection, the students explain the change that occurred, usually in the form of hypotheses or generalizations.

FIGURE 10.4 Inquiry Training Model

descends to the bottom of the bottle undamaged. She then invites students to ask her questions about what they observed, what scientific principles they could apply to this demonstration, and, finally, what they thought happened to the egg, the fire, and the bottle.

This particular demonstration and others like it allow the teacher to have considerable control over the structure and process of the lesson, but they also allow students the opportunity to construct alternative explanations while helping them apply abstract concepts. The teacher retains the role of "expert" but simultaneously guides the students to a level of expertise through inquiry and discovery. The model uses a traditional strategy, the classroom demonstration, but allows for considerable exploration of that demonstration in a constructivist environment. Finally, it enables students to recapture some of the natural curiosity and inquisitiveness that might have been lost in more didactic lessons.

Figure 10.4 summarizes the Inquiry Training Model and illustrates the three phases that make up the key elements of the model.

THE SYNECTIC MODEL

The Synectic Model was developed by William Gordon, an advertising executive, who frequently found that he and his colleagues would hit a "creative block" that would stymie their ability to design effective ads. In 1961, he wrote *Synectics: The Development of Creative Capacity* in response to a perceived need to reinvigorate the imagination and creating thinking that characterizes childhood but declines rapidly throughout adolescence and into adulthood. Gordon believed that people could be taught to think more creatively through the use of analogies and exercises that would stimulate the imagination. He developed three types of analogies: the personal analogy, the direct analogy, and the compressed conflict. While using these analogies, people would employ three Synectic exercises: stretching, exploring the unfamiliar, and creating something new (Gunter et al., 2003, pp. 137–144; Joyce, Weil, & Calhoun, 2004, pp. 155–186).

Thinking analogically through personal and direct analogies involves students in using metaphors to a greater extent than is typical in most classrooms. In a traditional, teacher-directed lesson at a lower cognitive level, for example, students tend to think using logical, rational strategies to organize and memorize information to respond accurately and correctly. In a Synectic Model, however, students are invited and encouraged to think analogically and nonrationally to break through the constraints of traditional thought. Using the Synectic Model, teachers can stimulate creative thinking in virtually every content area.

The three types of analogies, the personal analogy, direct analogy, and compressed conflict (or symbolic analogy) (Gunter et al., 2003, p. 136), can be used to teach specific concepts and skills, or they can be used more generally to stimulate creative thinking. The following examples use the three types of analogies with specific concepts. The personal analogy uses the Synectic exercise of "exploring the unfamiliar." The direct analogy employs the "stretching" exercise, and the compressed conflict involves "creating something new."

The personal analogy involves the students in actually becoming, analogically, the concept or skill they are to learn. For example, if an auto mechanics class were learning how an internal combustion engine worked, the students would each take on the role of an engine part to show the four stages of an internal combustion engine. If a science class were learning the concept of the expansion and contraction of a metal object, the students could represent molecules in the object and demonstrate how they would move as they got hotter (expansion) and colder (contraction). Finally, in a language arts class, some students would be given words that represent a part of speech while others would be given punctuation marks. They would then be asked to locate the appropriate words and punctuation marks that would allow them to create a complete, grammatically correct sentence. Such personal analogies would be most effective when teaching an abstract, difficult-to-visualize concept or skill or one that was not inherently interesting to the students, or possibly both.

The direct analogy involves taking the attributes of one concept and using them to illustrate the attributes of another more abstract or difficult concept. This requires the students to stretch their imaginations through the use of similes and metaphors. For example, in a social studies class, students could be asked to compare the various systems of the human body (for example, circulation, skeletal, central nervous systems) to the various systems or functions of society (for example, transportation, economic, communication systems) to familiarize them with the interconnectedness of systems in both contexts. The problem with direct analogies and with metaphors in general is that the attributes have to be congruent or the analogy breaks down. A faulty analogy can create a misconception in the same way that a poorly chosen set of examples can cause students to focus on the noncriterial attributes of a concept rather than the criterial attributes.

The compressed conflict, or symbolic analogy, uses apparently contradictory concepts to create a new concept. As Gunter et al. (2003, p. 136) point out, while this appears to be similar to an oxymoron in using contradictory terms, the compressed conflict is more insightful creatively. Citing the political columnist William Safire, they identify several examples of compressed conflicts, including open secret, cruel kindness, deliberate speed, and deafening silence (p. 136). These examples suggest that compressed conflicts expand and extend thinking by creating something new and revealing.

Three Kinds of Analogies

1. Personal analogy: The students *become* the object or phenomenon they are studying.
2. Direct analogy: The students draw comparisons between (or among) apparently unlike objects or events.
3. Compressed conflict: The students combine two seemingly contradictory words or phrases thus creating a new concept.

Three Typical Synectic Exercises

1. Stretching
2. Exploring the unfamiliar
3. Creating something new

FIGURE 10.5 The Synectic Model

Students could be given an example of a compressed conflict—for example, a benevolent dictator—and then asked to identify individuals throughout history who would fit that concept and to explain why that term would fit. Or students could be asked to provide examples of compressed conflicts that they have heard or read about and then have them analyze these terms to determine if they are humorous or ironic terms (for example, jumbo shrimp or military intelligence) or if they create a new insight on a phenomenon (for example, organized chaos or nourishing flame).

In each of these examples, students must expand and extend their thinking beyond the logical and sequential strategies encountered in lessons with a specific, defined concept or skill to be learned. The Synectic Model forces the students and the teacher to recapture the "creative imaginings" exhibited by young children as they engage in play and fantasy. Using the three types of analogies and exercises summarized in Figure 10.5 will facilitate this process and provide a helpful structure for designing lessons and selecting activities that will encourage creative thought.

THE SELF-DIRECTED LEARNING MODEL

Self-directed learning (SDL) provides students with the opportunity to plan, implement, and assess their own learning through individual and group projects. This model draws heavily upon the constructivist philosophy as students take responsibility for setting and meeting learning outcomes they believe will best meet their learning needs. Proponents of self-directed learning stress the importance of the contextual nature of learning and identify five characteristics that differentiate self-directed learning from teacher-directed learning:

1. Self-directed learning recognizes that students have an innate need to exercise control over their own lives. Teacher-directed learning assumes that students are essentially dependent; the teacher decides what is to be taught, when, and how.

2. Self-directed learning is based on the belief that as the learner grows in experience, he or she becomes a major resource for determining future learning, and this resource should be used along with textbooks and other resources. Teacher-directed learning depicts the student's experience as less valuable than the teacher's.

3. Self-directed learning regards learners as so individual in development that each is ready to learn what is essential to perform the tasks she/he has chosen to fulfill a perceived need. Teacher-directed learning believes that students mature at varying times, but at times have common characteristics and learning needs and can be grouped for teaching purposes.

4. Self-directed learning says that the subject matter orientation stifles learner initiative and that the natural way of learning immerses students in problem-centered experiences, personal projects, and current needs, thus helping them master daily problems. Teacher-directed learning provides a subject-centered orientation to learning; learning experiences are organized according to the respective disciplines. Lessons, units, and tests become the focal point of teaching.

5. Self-directed learning is based on the belief that internal incentives—native curiosity, the need for self-esteem, the challenge of power, the satisfaction of accomplishment, and fulfillment—are the best motivators of student accomplishment. Teacher-directed learning views students as needing external incentives to learn. Punishment, force, grades, and diplomas are needed to keep children on the task and learning (ERS Bulletin, 1997, pp. 1–2).

Both Patricia Cross (1981) and Malcolm Knowles (1975) further support these characteristics by stating that approximately 70 percent of adult learning is self-directed (Cross, 1981) and that self-directed learning requires the learner to diagnose learning needs, formulate learning goals, identify resources for learning, select and implement learning strategies, and evaluate learning outcomes (Knowles, 1975). Knowles's description of the SDL process closely approximates the "Project Method" that William H. Kilpatrick first described in the 1920s (Cremin, 1964). In the Project Method, as in Knowles's description of SDL, the student is the primary source and resource for learning, and the teacher's role becomes that of guide or additional resource person. If necessary, the teacher can also assist in clarifying the purpose and objectives for the project, suggesting additional resources or experiences, and providing an external perspective for purposes of assessment.

Because the teacher's role in the SDL Model is significantly different from that in the other models discussed in this chapter, the process for instructional design for this model is different as well. In Figure 10.6, the Self-Directed Learning Model essentially combines the Project Method of Kilpatrick and the SDL process described by Knowles. More than any other model, the Self-Directed Learning Model basically establishes a learning environment that enables students to design instruction rather than the teacher. The teacher's responsibility is to create the environment and ensure that students follow the process outlined

Phase One:	Learners diagnose their own learning needs.
Phase Two:	Learners formulate a set of learning outcomes that address the needs identified.
Phase Three:	Learners identify resources for learning.
Phase Four:	Learners select and implement learning experiences and strategies.
Phase Five:	Learners evaluate learning outcomes through self-assessment and/or external assessments based on established criteria.

FIGURE 10.6 The Self-Directed Learning Model

to reach the learning outcomes. To do this successfully, the teacher must assist the students in connecting their projects to the projects of other students and, ultimately, to both the established and the emergent curriculum.

USING THE MODELS OF TEACHING EFFECTIVELY

The models of teaching selected as representing a contextual approach for creating holistic learning environments in the classroom connect well-researched theories of teaching and learning to a "best practices" approach to instructional design. Ultimately, however, the effectiveness of this approach rests upon the teacher who must make the decisions necessary to implement these practices. Not every unit planning, lesson planning, and teaching model will work for every teacher unless that teacher perceives a correlation between the models and his or her personal theories of teaching and learning. Developing a repertoire of teaching strategies and models is essential for effective teaching, but the strategies and models must be consistent with the teacher's style, which is a manifestation of his or her philosophy of teaching and learning.

The models of teaching simply provide a guiding structure for the teacher to follow when planning instruction and to compare against when analyzing the lesson's effectiveness following instruction. The models empower the teacher to design learning environments that can foster contextual teaching and learning and achieve the results indicated by the research that supports CTL. As students and teachers find themselves functioning more and more in an information-rich, technologically driven, rapidly changing world, the importance of being able to think and act successfully in a variety of contexts increases dramatically. The models that enable students to experience these contexts both within and outside the formal classroom should also encourage students to apply their learning to new and unanticipated contexts. This is the essence of contextual teaching and learning as a philosophy and a practice that empowers teachers and students to "have the ability and desire to learn and solve problems in a variety of complex contexts throughout their lifetimes" (Howey, 1998, p. 20).

REFERENCES

Cremin, L. (1964). *The transformation of the school.* New York: Vintage Books.

Cross, K. P. (1981). *Adults as learners.* San Francisco: Jossey-Bass.

DeMar, G. (1997, April). Behaviorism. Retrieved November 9, 2002, from http://forerunner.com/forerunner/X04497_DeMar_-Behaviorism.html

ERS Bulletin. (1997, January). *Self-directed learning, 24*(5). Retrieved September 20, 2003, from http://www.ers.org/ERSbulletins/0197c.htm

Gunter, M. A., Estes, T., & Schwab, J. (2003). *Instruction: A models approach* (4th ed.). Boston: Pearson.

Henriques, L. (2002, May). *Constructivist teaching and learning.* Retrieved December 9, 2003, from http://www.edu.uvic.ca/depts/snsc/temporary/cnstrct.htm

Howey, K. (1998). Introduction to the commissioned papers. In K. Howey (Ed.), *Contextual teaching and learning: Preparing teachers to enhance student success in and beyond school* (p. 20). Columbus, OH: ERIC Clearinghouse on Adult, Career and Vocational Education.

Joyce, B., & Weil, M. (1972). *Models of teaching.* Englewood Cliffs, NJ: Prentice Hall.

Joyce, B., & Weil, M., & Calhoun, E. (2004). *Models of teaching* (7th ed.). Boston: Pearson.

Knowles, M. (1975). *Self-directed learning: A guide for learners and teachers.* New York: Association Press.

APPENDIX A

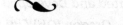

Sample Curriculum
Designs

CURRICULUM DESIGN

Created and Developed by Julie Ford
Oregon (OH) City Schools

STATEMENT OF PURPOSE

According to the American School Counselor Association, one in four children is bullied and one in five children engages in bullying behavior, while the National Schools Safety Center estimates that 2.7 million children are victims of bullying every year. A few researchers, however, have found that up to 80 percent of children are bullied during their school careers (Maine Project Against Bullying, 2000). Whether it is physical, verbal, or emotional abuse, bullying is aggressive behavior that is deliberate, repetitive, and hurtful.

Violence is increasing in our schools and in society as a whole. Bullying behavior is one predictor of future aggression, and studies have shown that there is a strong correlation between bullying and criminal activity. The National Education Association, for example, estimates that one in four bullies in school will have a criminal record by age 30. Because aggressive behavior is learned early and becomes resistant to change, a bullying unit at the elementary level is imperative. By teaching students how to prevent and respond to bullying, they will not only be able to reduce its occurrence at school but also take that knowledge and skill into their homes and communities, contributing to a safer society.

Because bullying affects everyone—victims, bullies, and bystanders—an understanding of and skills to prevent and respond to it are important for students to possess. Victims, for example, often experience physical, emotional, and behavioral problems and may also be at risk for committing suicide or engaging in violent acts themselves. Victims may also be unable to concentrate in school because their attention is drawn away from learning, resulting in a drop in academic performance. As fear increases, so do absences, truancy, and dropout rates. In fact, the National Education Association estimates that 160,000 students miss school every day because of bullying. Along with victims, however, bystanders also suffer as a result of bullying. The school climate, for example, can become negative and frightening, interfering with student learning and achievement. Bystanders may feel fearful and unsafe in school while others may learn that bullying is acceptable behavior and, at some point, even begin to engage in it themselves.

A bullying unit must be implemented so that students have the opportunity to grow, learn, and develop to their full potential. As a result of this unit, students will learn the concepts, skills, and strategies that will help them effectively respond to and prevent bullying, creating a safe and welcoming school environment for all students.

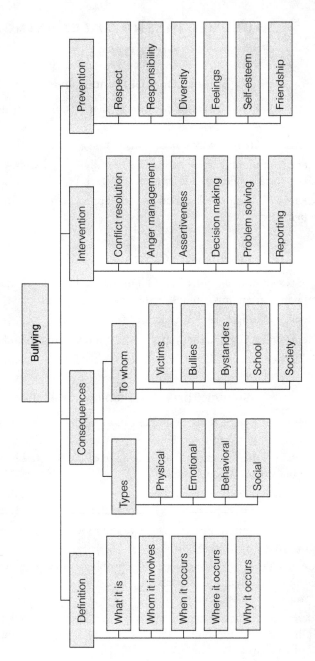

Bullying Concept Map

SUBUNIT INTENDED LEARNING
OUTCOMES

Subunit One: Defining Bullying

- Students will define bullying, including what it is, whom it involves, and when and where it occurs.
- Students will analyze why bullying occurs.
- Students will identify three categories of bullying—physical, verbal, and indirect/social—and provide examples of each type.
- Students will recognize that bullying is inappropriate, hurtful, and unacceptable behavior.

Subunit Two: Consequences of Bullying

- Students will describe the physical, emotional, behavioral, and social effects of bullying on victims, bullies, bystanders, school, and society.
- Students will empathize with victims' feelings.
- Students will recognize the importance of intervening in and preventing bullying.

Subunit Three: Intervening in Bullying

- Students will recognize that conflict can be resolved without resorting to bullying. (comprehension)
- Students will demonstrate the effective use of conflict resolution strategies in a bullying situation. (application)
- Students will recognize that anger can be a normal and healthy feeling but that some ways of expressing anger are better than others. (comprehension)
- Students will demonstrate the effective use of anger management strategies in a bullying situation. (application)
- Students will recognize the need for a problem-solving process in bullying situations, including the importance of involving everyone in the situation in the process. (comprehension)
- Students will demonstrate the effective use of a problem-solving process, including identifying solutions that are acceptable to everyone involved in the bullying situation. (application)
- Students will recognize the need for decision-making skills in bullying situations, including the importance of obtaining information from those whom the decision will affect. (comprehension)
- Students will demonstrate the effective use of decision-making skills in a bullying situation. (application)

- Students will recognize the differences among aggressive, passive, and assertive behaviors and the effectiveness of using assertiveness in a bullying situation. (comprehension)
- Students will demonstrate the effective use of assertive behavior in a bullying situation. (application)
- Students will recognize the importance of reporting bullying. (comprehension)
- Students will demonstrate effective reporting techniques in a bullying situation. (application)

Subunit Four: Preventing Bullying

- Students will demonstrate an appreciation for diversity.
- Students will recognize, empathize with, and validate others' feelings.
- Students will demonstrate respect for others.
- Students will describe ways to increase self-esteem of self and others.

SEQUENCING RATIONALE

This bullying unit is organized according to the concept-related pattern of logical prerequisite. Although several patterns could have been used in sequencing the four subunits that compose this unit, the content appears to be best presented in the logical prerequisite pattern because it provides a way of ordering concepts that makes the most sense for students.

The first subunit, "Defining Bullying," is the most logical starting point for students to learn about bullying because they must first understand what it is and be able to identify it when they experience it or observe it taking place. This subunit will provide the knowledge base that students will need to understand and appreciate the remainder of the unit.

The next subunit, "Consequences of Bullying," is appropriate because it will help students recognize the seriousness of bullying as well as tap into the affective domain. By helping students empathize with victims, as well as recognize the harm bullying does not only to victims but also to bystanders, school, and community, it is expected that students will become interested in and motivated to reduce and, if possible, eliminate bullying.

The third subunit, "Intervening in Bullying," is logically sequenced at this point because it is when students will most likely desire to learn how to intervene in bullying situations. This unit will not only help victims learn how to handle bullying situations that require immediate intervention but will also teach bystanders how to assist victims under these circumstances.

The final subunit, "Preventing Bullying," is appropriate because students by this time will understand what bullying is, its consequences, and how to prevent it and will now be concerned with preventing it from occurring. This subunit will also help students create a safe and welcoming school environment, improve their self-esteem, appreciate the diversity that exists around them, and, ultimately, enhance student learning.

EVALUATION STRATEGY

Both formative and summative evaluation methods will be used to appraise the strengths and weaknesses of the bullying curriculum. The school counselor, who usually has contact with the entire staff, could conduct part of the formative evaluation by obtaining feedback from these individuals regarding what knowledge and skills they believe a bullying curriculum should cover based on student need. Because teachers, aids, and other staff members often have more chances to observe students than the counselor does, they could provide valuable information pertaining to curriculum evaluation. Teachers may also observe classroom guidance lessons to identify what students are learning and then provide feedback on whether or not they see students applying this information in other areas, such as in the classroom or on the playground.

Because the subject of bullying has recently received much attention from the media, many books, articles, workshops, and lectures are being offered to educate teachers, counselors, and parents on this topic. To learn more about bullying, stay current on the topic, and identify how others are addressing bullying in the schools, the counselor should engage in professional development activities, which will further assist him or her in evaluating the curriculum.

Pre- and postassessment surveys could provide yet another method of evaluation. Before conducting the unit, students could be given a survey measuring what they know about bullying, how they handle it, and how frequently they observe or experience it. Following the completion of the unit, a second survey could be administered to determine if any changes—positive or negative—had occurred since the bullying curriculum was implemented.

Performance-based assessments could also be used to evaluate the curriculum. Authentic assessments such as role playing and naturalistic observations would provide students with opportunities to demonstrate skills that have been identified as intended learning outcomes. Interviews and discussions with students could provide yet another method of obtaining information about the effectiveness of the curriculum.

In addition to these formative evaluation procedures, a summative evaluation could be conducted over the next three to five years using pre- and postassessment surveys. By measuring, assessing, and evaluating the results of the curriculum over an extended time period, the counselor and others could determine if the bullying unit should be continued, adapted, and/or altered to best meet the needs of students.

CURRICULUM DESIGN

Created and Developed by Katie Ryan
Southwestern City Schools, Columbus, OH

STATEMENT OF PURPOSE

Democracy in the United States is in disrepair. There is apathy, as shown in low voter turnout, and skepticism has risen regarding the effectiveness of voting methods in recent elections with recounts and recalls becoming necessary. National politics are often conducted by mass media commercials that are sometimes of questionable integrity, and local government has been viewed as hindered by gridlock and feuds. This state of democracy has citizens questioning the strength of our government. While many doubt or complain about our system, democracy for the most part works; it's the citizens who aren't participating in the government. Most of us can explain the theories of democracy, such as checks and balances, and how a bill becomes a law; however, few of us actually vote or voice our opinions to our city council or representatives. As a nation, we are failing to be a part of the democratic process.

Often our schools prepare students to understand citizenship, but not to act as citizens (America's Promise, 1998). We teach students the basic facts of democracy so they can pass standardized tests, but we do not teach them the necessary skills to be an active citizen. The following analogy illustrates this problem: if we taught driver's education in the same manner we teach citizenship in school, the course would include physics of combustion, history of the automobile, and theory of highway design. After a multiple-choice test, students would get their licenses and start driving. However, society demands that driver's education include a hands-on component. Shouldn't citizenship education also be hands on? Citizenship, like driving, is not a spectator sport (America's Promise, 1998).

I propose to enhance the Middle School Social Studies curriculum by adding a hands-on unit that promotes competent and responsible participation of students as citizens in the democratic process. This program will help young people to think critically and learn how to monitor and influence public policy, while developing an understanding of democratic values and principles. The students will learn to interact with their government through: identifying a problem in their community that requires a solution, gathering and evaluating information on the problem, examining and evaluating alternative solutions, developing a proposed public policy to address the problem, and developing an action plan to get their policy adopted by government.

This curriculum is consistent with the National Social Studies Content Standards and the Ohio Social Studies Standards. According to the National Council for the Social Studies (NCSS), the purpose of social studies is "to help young people develop the ability to make informed and reasoned decisions for the public good as citizens" (NCSS, 1994). The council states that social studies programs have a responsibility to promote civic competence—which is the knowledge, skills, and attitudes required of students to be able to assume the office of citizen (NCSS, 1994).

The Ohio Social Studies Standards state that by the end of the 6–8 program, students should be able to show the relationship between civic participation and attainment of civic and public goals as well as explain how people influence the government (Ohio Department of Education, 2003, p. 138). Students are also to work effectively in groups, take a position and support it with evidence, and analyze different perspectives on topics (ODE, 2003, p. 139). Hence, the proposed hands-on citizenship curriculum is well supported by both state and national standards.

It is imperative that this curriculum be added to the existing social studies program so that we can better prepare our students to think critically and to be active citizens who participate in the democratic process. In the last presidential election, only 39 percent of the registered electorate actually participated. The majority in that election were the people who didn't vote at all, not the Republicans, and not the Democrats. They argue about who's really the number one party. The number one party in American is the party of nonparticipation (America's Promise, 1998). It is so vital that we provide our students with the necessary tools so they can share their voice, help better our communities, and become the active citizens upon which our democracy was founded.

REFERENCES

America's Promise. (1998). *The America's promise teaching guide.* Los Angeles: Farmers Group.

National Council for the Social Studies. (1994). *Expectations of excellence: Curriculum standards for social studies.* Silver Springs, MD: Author. Retrieved February 1, 2004, from http://www.ncss.org/standards/stitle.html

Ohio Department of Education. (2003). *Academic content standards for social studies.* Columbus, OH: Author.

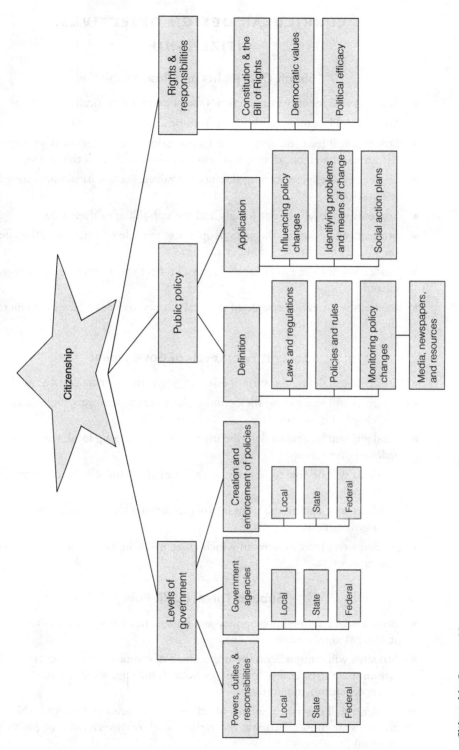

Citizenship Concept Map

CURRICULAR DESIGN OBJECTIVES:
CITIZENSHIP

Subunit One: Rights and Responsibilities

- Students will identify characteristics for obtaining American citizenship.
- Students will examine what it means to be an American citizen.
- Students will read and analyze the Constitution and the Bill of Rights to determine the rights, duties, and responsibilities of American citizens.
- Students will explore various democratic values, such as freedom, equality, and justice.
- Students will evaluate our society and the upholding of these values.
- Students will examine the ways people play the role of citizen and the effect they have on upholding democratic ideals.
- Students will define political efficacy and reflect upon their current role as a citizen.
- Students will develop a sense of political efficacy and describe ways to increase the efficacy of others.

Subunit Two: Levels of Government

- Students will define the various levels of government: federal, state, and local.
- Students will understand the defining characteristics, powers, and duties of each level of government.
- Students will be able to describe the relationship among local, state, and federal governments.
- Students will be able to distinguish the similarities and differences among the three levels.
- Students will analyze the need for balance among the national, state, and local government.
- Students will identify ways in which citizens can influence all three levels of government.

Subunit Three: Public Policy

- Students will define public policy and be able to identify various examples of it. (knowledge, comprehension)
- Students will comprehend the importance of monitoring policies and will demonstrate their ability to monitor policies through various avenues. (comprehension, application)
- Students will describe methods of influencing policies and analyze which methods are most effective at the various levels of government. (application, analysis)

- Students will identify problems at the local, state, and national level that need addressing. (comprehension)

- Students will identify a problem of their choice in their community to study. (application)

- Students will determine which level of government is directly responsible for dealing with this problem. (application)

- Students will research this problem, gathering and evaluating information about the problem from a variety of sources. (application, evaluation)

- Students will examine public policies that are currently being used by the government, and other agencies, and evaluate their effectiveness. (analysis, evaluation)

- Students will brainstorm and develop a creative solution to the problem by developing their own public policy. (synthesis)

- Students will develop an action plan on how to influence the appropriate government or agency to adopt their proposed policy. (synthesis)

- Students will actively become citizens by creating social action projects that allow them to actively influence public policy and problem solve. (synthesis)

SEQUENCING RATIONALE

This citizenship unit is sequenced according to the concept-related sequencing pattern of logical prerequisite. Although multiple sequencing patterns could have been applied to the organization of this unit, the citizenship concepts taught in this unit will be most comprehensible to students by arranging them in logical order.

The first subunit, "Rights and Responsibilities," is a logical starting point for this unit, as students will explore the Constitution and Bill of Rights to understand the principles upon which our citizenship is founded, as well as our rights, responsibilities, and duties as citizens. This subunit will also explore democratic values we embody as citizens and the importance of political efficacy. This subunit provides a framework and foundation for students, so that they can understand the more complex structures and issues surrounding citizenship.

"Levels of Government," is the second subunit, in which students will explore the three levels of government—local, state, and federal—and how these three affect citizens and public policies. Students will be able to distinguish among the powers, duties, and characteristics of these three levels of government. Students will also identify ways in which citizens can influence all three levels of government through various agencies, which will allow students to better understand the importance of citizens monitoring and influencing policies produced by these governments.

The final subunit, "Public Policy," is appropriate because students will apply information learned in the previous two units, in order to fully comprehend public policy and students' roles as citizens in monitoring and influencing public policies. This subunit will empower students to identify problems and means of change in addressing issues in their lives. Students will plan and develop social action plans to participate as active citizens and implement policy changes. Hence, ultimately, the students will actively be engaged in the citizenship process.

EVALUATION STRATEGY

Our nation was founded upon democratic principles, one being active participation of all citizens. In these changing times, it is imperative that we teach our students the importance of citizenship and how they can impact public policies effectively making improvements in our communities. Hence, it is important to ensure that we are empowering our students with the most effective curriculum on citizenship. Therefore, this citizenship curriculum will be assessed using both formative and summative evaluation methods to ensure that our students receive the very best education.

Formative evaluation will be conducted in several ways. The teacher of the unit can administer pre- and postassessment surveys to determine student knowledge of citizenship, level of participation, and interest in monitoring and influencing public policies. Other social studies teachers, as well as other faculty members, and administrators can also observe lessons and the students' social action projects to monitor their learning and provide feedback to the teacher. The social action projects created by the students provide an authentic form of evaluation where students are becoming active citizens and influencing their communities; hence, an analysis of the projects themselves will provide wonderful insight into the effectiveness of the curriculum.

In addition to the above evaluation, the teacher of the unit can also participate in professional development opportunities, such as America's Promise and Project Citizen workshops, to collaborate with other professionals on ways to actively teach citizenship to students. This type of professional development may give the teacher more insights and information, which could be helpful in evaluating the curriculum.

Finally, in addition to the formative evaluation methods, a summative evaluation can be conducted in the next three to five years, using pre- and postsurveys administered to both students and faculty in the building. By assessing the learning of the students, evaluating the social action plans, and analyzing the feedback provided, this will allow the teacher to critically reflect upon the effectiveness of the citizenship unit to determine if it should be modified, adapted, or continued in its present state to best meet the needs of all students.

CURRICULUM DESIGN

Created and Developed by Nathan Ash
Van Buren High School, Van Buren, Ohio

CURRICULUM STATEMENT OF PURPOSE

When the State Board of Education changed the course requirements from two credits of high school science to three credits, Van Buren High School did not add any courses to its curriculum. Instead, students would have to get their third credit of science by taking a college preparatory chemistry course or by taking two years of agricultural science (each year counts as one half science credit). There are many problems with students trying to find a third course that fits their needs as well as satisfying the State's requirements. Because of this, I am writing a curriculum for a course that will fall somewhere between a college preparatory class and an agriculture science course. The course that I am proposing is a science and technology course that will give the students hands-on, minds-on activities that are based on real problems a technician might see in industry.

The Science and Technology course will be designed for students who either are interested in entering the workforce right after school or for those who are interested in getting a two-year degree and working in industry. This course will address societal needs by focusing the students' efforts in science toward something that is practical and relevant to a productive community. One of the main goals of the course is to emphasize the importance of science and technology in the workplace and ultimately how science and technology affects the community. Currently, no course taught at Van Buren covers the Ohio Science Standards from this angle.

Science and Technology will be developed with the intent of students using the knowledge acquired in the workplace. The real hook for why students would want to take the course will be because of its practicality. The answer for the age-old question of "Why do we need to know this?" will be very obvious to students because of the real-world applications that will be involved with the course. There will be a wide range of industries studied such as the carbonated beverage industry, paint industry, semiconductor industry, and forensic science. This will give the students a snapshot of some of the available areas they could pursue.

The content covered in this course will be consistent with the Ohio Science Model and much time will be devoted to showing the relationship between science and society. Since this course is being designed for a student's third science credit, then it will follow the science standards for the 11th and 12th grade. In particular, the Science and Technology standards, Scientific Inquiry standards, and Scientific Ways of Knowing standards will be met by this course.

The Science and Technology course will be a course that develops skills and concepts needed in today's industries. This course is a unique approach to teaching science content in a meaningful context.

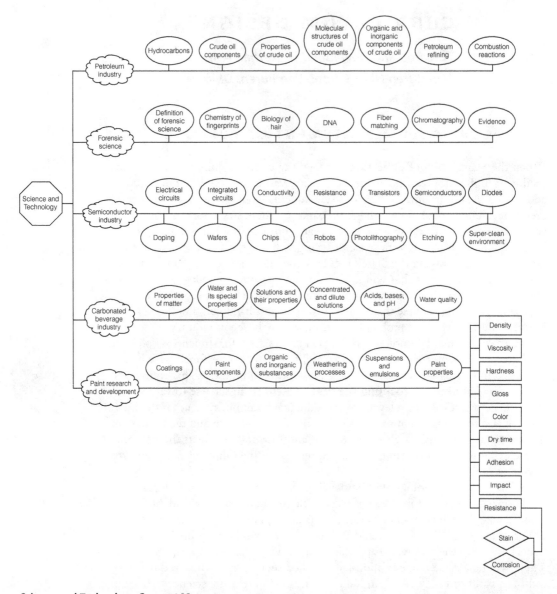

Science and Technology Concept Map

UNIT INTENDED LEARNING OUTCOMES

Forensic Science

- Students will be able to define forensic science and describe situations where forensic science can be used. (knowledge)
- Students will gather, analyze, and summarize evidence from the perspective of a forensic examiner. (application, analysis)

- Students will define chromatography. (knowledge)
- Students will explain how pigments are separated through capillary action. (comprehension)
- Students will demonstrate the ability to make chromatograms from known samples as well as collect evidence using proper laboratory techniques. (application)
- Students will analyze chromatograms for comparison with evidence. (evaluation)
- Students will demonstrate that they can set up fields in a database. (application)
- Students will construct a database using fields that they feel are integral in a descriptive record. (synthesis)
- Students will manage the database: entering data, sorting data, and searching for entries. (application)
- Students will demonstrate skills used to examine sample fibers through a microscope. (application)
- Students will identify visible characteristics of fibers under magnification. (analysis)
- Students will perform flame tests to identify chemical properties of heat resistance, flammability, and odor. (application)
- Students will classify fibers and compare to known fibers. (comprehension)
- Students will define the major fingerprint ridge patterns as whorls, loops, and arches. (knowledge)
- Students will identify the major patterns in fingerprint ridges such as whorls, loops, and arches for a fingerprint sample. (knowledge)
- Students will be able to collect fingerprints from suspects by using graphite and clear tape. (application)
- Students will isolate and identify ridge characteristics (hooks, eyes, end ridges, forks) on collected fingerprints. (analysis)
- Students will explain how characteristics of fingerprints can be used as forensic evidence. (comprehension)
- Students will use characteristics of the ridge patterns to match fingerprints. (evaluate)
- Students will use forensic evidence to argue a case against a suspect. (evaluation)

Carbonated Beverage Industry

- Students will explain how solutions are made and show how water plays a special role in these processes. (comprehension, application)
- Students will categorize matter as a mixture or a pure substance based on its chemical and physical properties. (comprehension)
- Students will differentiate between acids and bases by measuring the pH. (analysis)

- Students will be able to explain the difference in the properties of acids and bases. (application)
- Students will be able to explain the pH scale. (application)
- Students will be demonstrate they can make serial dilutions. (synthesis)
- Students will describe how a hydrometer is used to measure density of solutions. (application)
- Students will relate physical properties with varying concentrations of solutions. (comprehension)
- Students will calibrate a homemade hydrometer to the standard solutions already produced. (analysis)
- Students will create a calibration curve based on their hydrometer. (synthesis)
- Students will demonstrate that they can use the hydrometer along with their calibration curve to analyze the sugar content of solutions and determine unknown concentrations. (evaluation)
- Students will define the parts of a solution. (knowledge)
- Students will demonstrate that they can calculate mass percentages for solutions. (application)
- Students will make solutions of specified percent mass of solutes. (synthesis)
- Students will explain the difference between a dilute solution and a concentrated solution. (application)
- Students will define qualitative data. (knowledge)
- Students will compare color samples for "off-spec" determination of cola samples.
- Students will explain how human perception can affect decisions made in a quality control laboratory. (application)
- Students will identify regions of the tongue that are taste specific. (analysis)
- Students will define ions, hardness, polar molecules, solvents, solutes, and solutions. (knowledge)
- Students will explain why water is an excellent solvent based on its polarity. (comprehension)
- Students will analyze water samples for hardness, iron content, and chlorine content. (analysis)
- Students will relate the possible effects on taste of off-spec soda due to the content of ions. (evaluation)

Semiconductor Industry

- Students will define a wafer, chip, and integrated circuit and show how these three terms are related. (knowledge, comprehension)
- Students will analyze and identify the parts of an integrated circuit through the use of digital microscopy. (application)

- Students will create macroscopic electrical circuits using batteries, resistors, switches, LEDs, and transistors. (application)
- Students will demonstrate skills used to measure electrical properties of an electrical circuit using digital and computer-based multimeters. (application)
- Students will describe how electricity flows through various circuitry components, such as resistors, diodes, and transistors. (analysis)
- Students will be able to describe how an integrated circuit functions. (analysis)
- Students will identify the differences and similarities between a p-type and an n-type transistor. (comprehension)
- Students will model the processes of masking and doping in the fabrication of a microchip. (synthesis)
- Students will evaluate the cleanliness of a workplace and recognize the importance of clean environments in the fabrication of integrated circuits. (evaluation)
- Students will define how an assembly line process works and the importance of each step to the final product. (comprehension)

Paint Research and Development

- Students will identify the many properties that gives paint its functionality. (analysis)
- Students will identify and explain the factors that are taken into account when paint is developed. (application, analysis)
- Students will define adhesion and gloss in relation to paints. (knowledge)
- Students will explain procedures used to test paint samples for adhesion and gloss. (comprehension)
- Students will develop experiments to test properties of adhesion and gloss. (synthesis)
- Students will describe how polymers cross-link to become hardened when dry. (comprehension)
- Students will analyze data to determine hardness of paint. (analysis)
- Students will use information gathered in previous experiments to develop a paint. (synthesis)
- Students will design tests to analyze properties of the paint they developed. (evaluate)
- Students will describe both the positive and negative characteristics of the paint they developed. (evaluate)
- Students will analyze colors of paint. (analysis)
- Students will describe the color of paint as a physical property. (comprehension)

- Students will perform tests and make mixtures to color match a sample to a standard. (analysis)
- Students will define resins. (knowledge)
- Students will identify the common polymers that are used in the paint industry's resins. (knowledge)
- Students will describe physical and chemical properties of resins (viscosity, density, pH). (comprehension)
- Students will analyze physical and chemical properties of resins. (analysis)
- Students will create films for testing purposes. (application)

Petroleum Industry

- Students will define petroleum and the components of petroleum. (knowledge)
- Students will explain where petroleum is found. (comprehension)
- Students will defend the necessity of petroleum in society. (evaluation)
- Students will judge the impacts on the environment of using petroleum products. (evaluation)
- Students will read and interpret MSDSs for different substances. (analysis)
- Students will explain the necessity of MSDSs in a variety of industries. (application)
- Students will develop safety/health/environmental guidelines using MSDSs. (synthesis)
- Students will define solubility. (knowledge)
- Students will explain how mixtures can be separated by density differences. (comprehension)
- Students will determine the percent water in crude oil mixture. (analysis)
- Students will define density. (knowledge)
- Students will calculate density using mass and volume measurements. (application)
- Students will compare density measurements to identify substances. (analysis)
- Students will explain why different ions produce different colors when heated. (comprehension)
- Students will create flame test standards using known ions. (synthesis)
- Students will compare flame test results with standard colors to identify ions present in a solution. (analysis)
- Students will explain that sulfur compounds corrode metals. (application)
- Students will analyze crude oil samples for sulfur content. (analysis)
- Students will define purity in terms of clarity of solutions. (knowledge)
- Students will design a flow diagram of tests and processes crude oil undergoes during refining. (synthesis)

SEQUENCING RATIONALE

The curriculum design for the Science and Technology course branches out into five major units that are similar in difficulty and are not directly related to or dependent upon each other. For these reasons, the units are not sequenced in a chronological order or in order of increasing difficulty. Instead, the course will be organized to the learning-related model of student interest. Since this course is designed for students who may have difficulty finding their niche in science, it is logical to approach the material from this viewpoint to encourage student excitement.

The first unit in the sequence of the course will be "Forensic Science." With the recent success of television shows that deal with the scientific side of crime investigation, it seems natural to present this material first. Students will become familiar with the laboratory equipment and procedures that will allow them to be successful in the units to follow. Also, the final project for this unit, investigating the evidence of a bank robbery, will lay the foundation of inquiry-based learning experiences that the students will encounter throughout the entire course.

The second unit will be the "Carbonated Beverage Industry" because of the practicality and familiarity of the topic. This unit will reinforce laboratory techniques and inquiry-based learning strategies while establishing a base for chemistry concepts for future units.

The next unit, "Semiconductor Industry," will strike some interest for students because they will be tearing apart computer chips and investigating how computers work at the microscopic level. This unit will be more complex because of the abstractness of microscopic science. Although many laboratory techniques learned in prior units will be utilized, there is a heavy emphasis on using new procedures to study the world of microtechnology.

The unit "Paint Research and Development" will be the fourth unit discussed because it is not as familiar to the majority of students. There are many properties of paint that will be defined and investigated, and the students will need to be well versed in using laboratory equipment. The final project of this unit is to use research and development to formulate a new paint that could be used in the automobile industry. Of the four units discussed up to this point, this final project requires the most scientific observation and investigation. Decisions must be based on empirical evidence, and the interrelatedness between properties must be carefully monitored to make the paint viable. Clearly, the students will need to build up their abilities to achieve this task.

Finally, the "Petroleum Industry" will be studied. This unit is last in the sequence because of the negative perceptions that surround the oil business, both social perceptions and scientific perceptions. The unit will be focused on investigating the many different uses of the various parts of crude oil. Through careful lab techniques, students will be able to identify different compounds of petroleum. Students will explore society's dependence on this natural resource while learning how emerging technology in waning industries such as the petroleum industry is driven by societal needs.

EVALUATION STRATEGY

The teacher and the curriculum director for the high school will conduct the majority of the evaluation of the Science and Technology course in the first year and subsequent years. In order for the course to meet the purpose of preparing students to work as technicians in industry, there needs to be a partnership with local businesses to be assured that the curriculum is in line with industrial needs. It would be reasonable to suggest that the teacher along with the curriculum director and local business leaders would be responsible for the formative evaluation of the curriculum.

The teacher could gather information from many different aspects to see if the curriculum is teachable material. Student portfolios could be generated for each industry unit and then student-led interviews could be used to gather data about student progress and understanding of the industry. This data can then be used to determine if the intended learning outcomes were appropriate. Also, students could be assigned final projects upon the completion of each unit that encompasses both the content and processes involved in the industry. This form of authentic assessment could be used to verify that students develop higher-order thinking skills that meet the intended learning outcomes geared toward scientific inquiry.

Teachers could administer pre- and postassessment surveys of each unit to students. Teachers, curriculum directors, and local business leaders could review the summaries of these surveys to evaluate student perceptions and misconceptions about the industry. Also, business leaders could review the intended learning outcomes for their specific industry and give feedback as to whether or not they are relevant. In combination with this, it could be very useful for the teacher to spend some time as a Co-Op in each of the industries to get a sense of the content and processes that are needed to be successful.

All of these formative evaluations should be followed up with summative evaluations in several years. Everyone involved must realize that this course is based on technology that is always changing and growing, therefore the curriculum must also be able to change and grow. Teaching methods and projects that work now may not work in five years. Realizing this is important for developing summative evaluation strategies because analyzing how the curriculum meets the needs of the students and their transition into the work force is as important as simply meeting the core content. To do this, there needs to be extensive dialogues among the school, industry, and students (both former and current).

Sample Instructional Designs

INSTRUCTIONAL SUBUNIT ON BULLYING

Created and Developed by Julie Ford
Oregon (OH) City Schools

UNIT OUTCOMES

Subunit One: Defining Bullying

- Students will define bullying, including what it is, whom it involves, and when and where it occurs.
- Students will analyze why bullying occurs.
- Students will identify three categories of bullying, physical, verbal, and indirect/social, and provide examples of each type.
- Students will recognize that bullying is inappropriate, hurtful, and unacceptable behavior.

Subunit Two: Consequences of Bullying

- Students will describe the physical, emotional, behavioral, and social effects of bullying on victims, bullies, bystanders, school, and society.
- Students will empathize with victims' feelings.
- Students will recognize the importance of intervening in and preventing bullying.

Subunit Three: Intervening in Bullying

- Students will recognize that conflict can be resolved without resorting to bullying. (comprehension)
- Students will demonstrate the effective use of conflict resolution strategies in a bullying situation. (application)
- Students will recognize that anger can be a normal and healthy feeling but that some ways of expressing anger are better than others. (comprehension)
- Students will demonstrate the effective use of anger management strategies in a bullying situation. (application)
- Students will recognize the need for a problem-solving process in bullying situations, including the importance of involving everyone in the situation in the process. (comprehension)

- Students will demonstrate the effective use of a problem-solving process, including identifying solutions that are acceptable to everyone involved in the bullying situation. (application)
- Students will recognize the need for decision-making skills in bullying situations, including the importance of obtaining information from those whom the decision will affect. (comprehension)
- Students will demonstrate the effective use of decision-making skills in a bullying situation. (application)
- Students will recognize the differences among aggressive, passive, and assertive behaviors and the effectiveness of using assertiveness in a bullying situation. (comprehension)
- Students will demonstrate the effective use of assertive behavior in a bullying situation. (application)
- Students will recognize the importance of reporting bullying. (comprehension)
- Students will demonstrate effective reporting techniques in a bullying situation. (application)

Subunit Four: Preventing Bullying

- Students will demonstrate an appreciation for diversity.
- Students will recognize, empathize with, and validate others' feelings.
- Students will demonstrate respect for others.
- Students will describe ways to increase self-esteem of self and others.

PRE-ASSESSMENT SURVEY: "WHAT I KNOW ABOUT BULLYING"

Circle the letter that best describes how you feel about the sentence:

A = Agree   D = Disagree   NS = Not Sure

1. Bullying can hurt victims' bodies and their feelings.	A	D	NS
2. Making fun of someone's clothes and hair is bullying.	A	D	NS
3. Some students deserve to be bullied.	A	D	NS
4. Bullying affects bullies, victims, and observers.	A	D	NS
5. Bullying can happen anywhere in school.	A	D	NS
6. Students who are bullied should fight back.	A	D	NS
7. Students who are bullied should ignore the bully.	A	D	NS

8. If you see someone being bullied, you should tell   A   D   NS
   the teacher.

9. If you see someone being bullied, it's okay to laugh.   A   D   NS

10. Victims of bullying may feel very sad and lonely.   A   D   NS

11. When I see someone being bullied, it bothers me.   A   D   NS

12. Fighting is the best way to solve an argument.   A   D   NS

13. What do you do when you get mad? How do you deal with your feelings?

    _____

14. If you are feeling sad, what do you do to help yourself feel better?

    _____

15. How can you help someone who is sad feel better?

    _____

16. How many times this week has a student tried to physically hurt you? _____

17. How many times this week have you tried to physically hurt another
    student?_____

18. How many times this week have you seen a student physically hurt another
    student?_____

19. How many times this week has a student hurt your feelings?_____

20. How many times this week have you hurt another student's feelings? _____

21. How many times this week have you seen a student hurt another student's
    feelings? _____

22. What would you like to learn about bullying?

    _____

    _____

    _____

LESSON: CONFLICT RESOLUTION

Objective: Students will demonstrate the effective use of conflict
                      resolution strategies in a bullying situation.

Concepts/Skills: ▪ Day 1: sharing, taking turns, listening, postponing
                      ▪ Day 2: empathizing, laughing, compromising, getting
                        help, apologizing

Materials:
- "Conflict Resolution Strategies" worksheet
- "Conflict Scenarios" worksheet

Procedures:

Introductory Activity

Ask students to identify recent conflicts they have had with others and how they handled these situations. Encourage students to evaluate their effectiveness in dealing with conflict in these examples, and help students see the need they may have for learning more effective conflict resolution strategies.

Developmental Activity

- Discuss the first four conflict resolution strategies during the first lesson and the other five strategies during the following lesson. Ask students to read out loud the definition of each strategy then describe how the accompanying illustration depicts that strategy. Students can make up a variety of stories based on each picture and should try to explain why specific strategies may have been used. After volunteers read each strategy, explore with students the times they have used the strategy, the consequence of using the strategy, and what they might have done differently in that particular situation. The teacher should also provide additional examples of the strategy in use. Continue this process until all the strategies for the day have been discussed.

- Randomly assign students to groups of three or four. Give each group a scenario (cut the "Conflict Scenarios" worksheet into strips), and ask each group to decide on a strategy they would use. Give students a few minutes to practice acting out the scenario, then have each group act out the scene using the strategy that was selected. As each group finishes, encourage the other students to guess which strategy was used and to evaluate the effectiveness and appropriateness of that choice. Ask students to provide constructive feedback that is stated positively.

Concluding Activity

Process the lesson, asking questions such as:

- What strategy do you feel the most/least comfortable using? Why?

- If you could act out your scenario again, what would you do the same? What would you do differently? Why?

- When would you most likely use each particular strategy? Provide at least one example of when you might use each strategy.
- How did it feel to act out the part of the bully/bystander/victim?
- What was it like working with your group members?
- What was the most difficult part of this activity? What went the smoothest? Did you use any of the strategies we talked about today in your group? If so, which did you use and why?
- What did you learn from today's lesson?

Evaluation: For homework, students will write out a short script about a bullying situation using one of the conflict resolution strategies discussed in class. During the next class, students will have the opportunity to act out their scripts for the class, and the other students will have the chance to guess what strategy was used and to evaluate the effectiveness of the strategy selected. Suggestions for other possible ways of handling the situation should also be encouraged.

Conflict Scenarios

1. You are in the lunch line. A bully cuts in front of you and then trips you as you walk to your seat.
2. You are waiting for the bus when a bully walks by and shoves you. You drop your books and bump your head.
3. A student steals your lunch money.
4. Someone calls you a name in the restroom.
5. A student puts you down in front of your classmates.
6. Students on the bus throw spitballs in your hair and call you names.
7. In gym class, you are always one of the last kids to be chosen for a team. When you end up on a team, several students begin to complain.
8. Your teacher asks a question. You know the answer, so you quickly raise your hand. A few students giggle and whisper after you respond.

Conflict Resolution Strategies

1. Share
Whatever the conflict is over, each person keeps or uses some of it.

2. Take turns
Let everyone get a chance to use or do something!

3. Listen
Try to understand the other person's feelings and ideas by really listening carefully.

4. Postpone
If someone is upset or tired, take a time out. Try to resolve the conflict later when everyone feels better.

5. Empathize
Put yourself in the other person's shoes. Try to see his or her side of the story.

6. Laugh
Try to laugh at the situation. A sense of humor helps everyone feel better!

8. Get help
Seek help with the situation from another student or an adult. It's okay to ask for help!

7. Compromise
Each person gives up part of what he or she wants so everybody can win!

9. Apologize
Accept responsibility for your part in the conflict. Say you are sorry for the situation.

LESSON: DECISION MAKING

Objective: Students will demonstrate the effective use of a decision-making process in a bullying situation.

Concepts/Skills: Decision-making steps, including: (1) identifying the problem, (2) brainstorming ways to solve the problem, (3) considering the consequences of each solution, and (4) choosing the best solution

Materials:
- "Decision-Making Steps" worksheet
- "Practicing Decision-Making Skills" worksheet
- "Decision-Making Scenario" worksheet

Procedures:

Introductory Activity

Ask students to describe times when they have made decisions and how they went about making those decisions. Encourage students to share the outcomes of their decisions, how they might have changed the way they made their decisions, and what they learned from their experiences.

Developmental Activity

- Tell the students that they are going to learn a way of making decisions, and explain that this information will help them decide which conflict resolution strategy to use in a bullying situation.
- Talk through the worksheet entitled, "Decision-Making Steps."
- Ask students to take turns reading out loud the situations on the worksheet, "Practicing Decision-Making Skills." Help the students use the decision-making model to make a decision in each of the four situations.
- Randomly assign students to groups of three or four. Ask each group to identify a decision that at least one of the members has had to make, preferably in regards to a bullying situation they may have experienced or observed, and ask each group to use the decision-making steps to choose the best possible conflict resolution strategy. When the groups have had enough time to go through the process and make their decisions, ask each group to explain the situation and the

decision-making process the group used. Encourage other students to comment on the effectiveness of the decision-making process used by the group, as well as to provide suggestions of other possible strategies that could have been used in that particular situation.

Concluding Activity

Process the lesson, asking questions such as:

- What steps in the decision-making process were the easiest for you? Which were the most difficult? Why?
- If you could go through the decision-making process again with the same scenario, what would you do the same? What would you do differently?
- What was it like working with your group members? What was the toughest part for your group? What went the most smoothly? Why?
- Have you used part(s) of this decision-making process before? If so, describe the situation, the step(s) you used, why you used the step(s), and what you might do differently now that you know this process.
- What did you learn from today's lesson?

Some key points to highlight during the processing of the activity include:

- Before you make a decision, you have to know your choices.
- What you know and what you like and dislike affect your decisions.
- Every decision has risks.
- The more important a decision, the more time you may need to make it.

Evaluation: Students will complete the homework assignment, the "Decision-Making Scenario" worksheet. During the next lesson, students will discuss the decisions they have made, their decision-making processes, the results of their decisions, the effectiveness of the process, and, if appropriate, how and why they might change their decisions.

Practicing Decision-Making Skills

Making decisions can be difficult. Because we make many decisions every day, it is important to use good decision-making skills. The more we practice considering options and choosing from choices, the better we will become at making even the toughest of decisions.

The children below have some difficult decisions to make. Help them make these tough decisions by using the four steps listed below:

1. Identify the problem.
2. Brainstorm ways to solve the problem.
3. Consider the consequences of each solution.
4. Choose the best solution.

Decision-Making Scenario

Draw a picture of the decision you need to make.

```



```

1. What is the problem?

   _____

2. What are some ways to solve the problem?

   ▪ _____

   ▪ _____

   ▪ _____

3. What are the consequences of each solution?

   ▪ _____

   ▪ _____

   ▪ _____

4. What is the best solution?

   _____

LESSON: ANGER MANAGEMENT

Objective:	▪ Students will demonstrate the effective use of anger management strategies.
Concepts/Skills:	▪ Anger management strategies, some of which may include exercising, breathing deeply, drawing, writing, or talking to a friend about feelings
Materials:	▪ "Anger Management Strategies" worksheet
	▪ balloon

Procedures: *Introductory Activity*

- The teacher introduces the activity by telling the students that he/she is going to act out a short scene and that they are to try to identify how the teacher feels as well as how they know this. The teacher then performs a short role play, acting as though he/she is very angry and demonstrating this anger through actions such as yelling, stomping feet, kicking, punching, and making angry facial expressions.

- After acting out the scene, ask the students how they think the teacher felt and what signs helped them determine this.

Developmental Activity

- Ask students to think about times when they have been angry or when they have seen someone else who is angry and have them describe how that anger was expressed. List the ways people deal with anger on the chalkboard, and discuss the pros and cons of each strategy. Talk about what makes some ways of expressing anger better than others.

- Talk about why is it important to express anger rather than keeping it inside. Tell students the following story. As you do, begin to blow air into the balloon each time the world "inflate" appears in the story.

  > One morning, James sleeps through his alarm clock, and his mom yells at him for not getting out of bed right away (inflate). When James gets to the kitchen, he finds out that someone finished all of his favorite cereal (inflate). James then misses the bus (inflate) and gets wet because it starts to rain while he's walking to school (inflate). When James finally gets to school, his teacher becomes upset because he is late again (inflate). Finally, when James is playing basketball in gym class, a student bumps into him while trying to make a basket, and James falls down (inflate). A few students begin to laugh (inflate).

- Ask students what will happen if air keeps getting added to the balloon. Then, ask how this is like someone who becomes more and more angry. Help students understand that it is important to express their anger but to do so in a way that does not hurt anyone else or themselves.

- Discuss what the phrase "anger management strategy" means and provide students with a few examples of strategies such as hitting a pillow, taking a walk, or writing in a journal. Then, randomly assign students to groups of three or four. Ask each group to brainstorm at least 10 anger management strategies.

- Ask the groups to take turns sharing one anger management strategy at a time, and write down these ideas on the chalkboard. Continue the process until all answers have been shared.
- Pass out the "Anger Management Strategies" worksheet and discuss any strategies that have not yet been suggested.

Concluding Activity

Process the lesson, asking questions such as:

- What anger management strategies do you feel the most/least comfortable using? Why?
- Have you ever used any of the strategies we talked about today? If so, describe the situation and the strategy you used. Was the strategy effective? How did you feel when you used it? Would you choose a different strategy since taking part in this lesson?
- When would you most likely use some of these strategies? Why? What determines which strategy you will use?
- What was it like working with your group members? What part of the process went the most smoothly? What part was the most difficult?
- What did you learn from today's lesson?

Anger Management Strategies

- Cry, scream, or yell, but do so in a place where you will not disturb anyone.
- Walk away from the person or situation that's making you angry.
- Talk to someone about your angry feelings, such as a friend or parent.
- Breathe. Take slow, deep breaths.
- Count to 10 s-1-o-w-l-y, or even count to 100. Do it again if you need to do so.
- Exercise. Shoot some hoops. Take a bike ride. Jump up and down. Get active.
- Draw a picture of your anger or write down how you feel.
- Turn on some relaxing music.
- Think calm, peaceful, and happy thoughts.
- Try tensing, then relaxing every muscle in your body from your head to toes.

- Use self-talk, saying things like, "I am calm," and "I am in control."
- Concentrate on something else.
- Ask yourself "Why am I angry?" Maybe the person didn't mean to make you angry. Maybe it was an accident or a misunderstanding. Make sure you understand the situation.
- Try not to take things personally. Know that the whole world isn't again you.

LESSON: PEER MEDIATION

Objective: Students will demonstrate the effective use of a peer mediation process in a bullying situation.

Concepts/Skills: Peer mediation steps, including: (1) introduce yourself, (2) identify the problem, (3) brainstorm solutions, (4) evaluate the solutions, and (5) choose a solution

Materials:
- "Peer Mediation Steps" worksheet
- "Peer Conflict Scenarios" worksheet

Procedures: *Introductory Activity*
- Ask students if they have ever witnessed a conflict between two students and, if so, if they tried to help. Give students the opportunity to describe the situation, how they tried to mediate, how the conflict ended, and what they learned from the experience.
- Tell the students that today they are going to learn how to intervene in a bullying situation as a bystander. Explain that they will be learning how to be a mediator, or someone who helps others resolve conflicts.

Developmental Activity
- Have volunteers read the steps involved in the peer mediation process. Talk through each step with the class, explaining what each step involves.
- Describe the following conflict scenario to the class, and ask for two volunteers to act out the situation. The teacher then uses the peer mediation process with these students, talking through each step.

    Roger is yelling at Laura in the hallway. Laura had promised to bring a book to school that she had borrowed from Roger, but she forgot it for the fourth day in a row. Roger needs the book to finish a report that is due

> *tomorrow, and he is very mad. Laura feels terrible about forgetting the book, but she is also upset because Roger is embarrassing her in the hallway. Roger keeps yelling, and Laura looks ready to cry.*

■ Present the next conflict scenario to the class, and ask for two more volunteers to act out the scene. This time, help the class work through the peer mediation process.

> *Larry tells several people during recess that his mom heard that Ron's parents are getting a divorce. Someone tells Ron what Larry is saying and Ron gets very upset. He walks over to Larry and tells him to shut up about his parents. Larry says, "Make me!" and he shoves Ron to the ground. "You're a loser just like your parents," says Larry. "Your parents are probably getting a divorce because they're sick of you!"*

■ Assign students into groups of four, and give each group a conflict scenario. Ask the groups to read through the situation and decide on who will play the following roles: two students in conflict, the mediator, and the helper (a person who is going to help the mediator work through the process by reading the steps out loud).

■ When the groups are ready, ask one group at a time to act out the scenario for the class. After each scene, encourage observers to provide feedback to the group on what they observed and to make suggestions for improvement. Participants may also comment on the performance.

Concluding Activity

Process the lesson, asking questions such as:

■ What part of the process was the easiest or most comfortable for you in the role you played? What step was the most difficult or uncomfortable for you? Why?

■ If you could act out the scenario again, what would you do the same? What would you do differently? Why?

■ Have you ever used part of the peer mediation process before? Describe the situation, the step(s) you used, why you used the step(s), and what you might do different now that we have gone through the peer mediating process.

■ What was it like working with your group members? Did you use any of these steps when working with your group and, if so, which ones?

- Why is it important to identify the problem correctly, especially when you are the mediator?
- What can you do if one or both of the students in the conflict refuse to cooperate in the mediation process?
- What can you do if one of the students involved in the conflict starts to cry? What if one of the students gets very angry?
- What should you do if you are really good friends with one of the students involved in the conflict?

Peer Mediation Steps

1. *Introduce Yourself*
   - Introduce yourself as a mediator.
   - Ask the students if they would like your help solving the problem.
   - Ask for agreement to begin mediation.
2. *Identify the Problem*
   - Ask each person what happened and how he or she feels.
   - Ask questions if anything is unclear. Summarize what you hear.
   - Make sure both students agree on the problem.
3. *Brainstorm Solutions*
   - Ask each person what he or she could do to solve the problem.
   - List on paper as many solutions as students can identity.
4. *Evaluate the Solutions*
   - Discuss each alternative.
   - Identify the consequences of each solution for both students.
5. *Choose a Solution*
   - Help the students choose a solution that works for both of them.
   - Make sure both students agree to the solution.
   - Remind them of confidentiality.
   - Congratulate them for their efforts.

Conflict Scenarios for Peer Mediation

1. Jim is mad because Troy got a better grade than he did on a spelling test. When Jim sees Troy in the hall, he trips Troy. Troy falls, and his books fly everywhere. A few students begin to giggle, and Jim says, "What a klutz! Guess who's the loser now!" Troy is embarrassed and angry.
2. Carrie follows Jessica into the restroom and shoves Jessica. Carrie accuses Jessica of spreading rumors about her sister, but Jessica says she doesn't even know Carrie's sister. Carrie calls Jessica a "liar" and says that she will make Jessica sorry for talking about her sister.

3. Every day on your way to the bus stop, you see an older boy picking on a younger student. The older student, Dave, always takes Dillon's lunch and goes through Dillon's backpack and steals things. You are walking by again today, but this time you decide to help.

4. Bill is the biggest kid in the school, and everyone tries to avoid him. As you walk in the cafeteria, you see Bill knock Steve's lunch tray to the ground. Steve calls Bill a "big jerk," and Bill calls Steve a "wimp." You can't find a teacher around, so you decide to help.

5. Jill is practicing with a soccer ball during recess. John asks if he can play with her, but Jill says, "No, you never share the ball with me when I ask." John gets mad and tries to take the ball away from Jill. She tries to fight back, but John pushes her to the ground. Jill starts to cry.

6. Liz is writing a story using the computer. When she leaves, Shawn reads her story. When Liz comes back, she sees Shawn and is so upset that she calls him names and tries to push him out of the way. Shawn says, "No one wants to read your stupid story anyway," and he deletes her story from the computer.

POST-ASSESSMENT SURVEY: "WHAT I KNOW ABOUT BULLYING"

Circle the letter that best describes how you feel about the sentence.

A = Agree   D = Disagree   NS = Not Sure

1. Bullying can hurt victims' bodies and their feelings.	A	D	NS
2. Making fun of someone's clothes and hair is bullying.	A	D	NS
3. Some students deserve to be bullied.	A	D	NS
4. Bullying affects bullies, victims, and observers.	A	D	NS
5. Bullying can happen anywhere in school.	A	D	NS
6. Students who are bullied should fight back.	A	D	NS
7. Students who are bullied should ignore the bully.	A	D	NS
8. If you see someone being bullied, you should tell the teacher.	A	D	NS
9. If you see someone being bullied, it's okay to laugh.	A	D	NS
10. Victims of bullying may feel very sad and lonely.	A	D	NS
11. When I see someone being bullied, it bothers me.	A	D	NS
12. Fighting is the best way to solve an argument.	A	D	NS

13. What do you do when you get mad? How do you deal with your feelings?

    _____

14. If you are feeling sad, what do you do to help yourself feel better?

    _____

15. How can you help someone who is sad feel better? _____

16. How many times this week has a student tried to physically hurt you? _____

17. How many times this week have you tried to physically hurt another
    student?_____

18. How many times this week have you seen a student physically hurt another
    student?_____

19. How many times this week has a student hurt your feelings?_____

20. How many times this week have you hurt another student's feelings? _____

21. How many times this week have you seen a student hurt another student's
    feelings? _____

22. Was there anything that you would have liked to learn about bullying that
    was not discussed?

    _____

    _____

    _____

UNIT POST-ASSESSMENT:
"WHAT I KNOW ABOUT BULLYING"

1. Name four conflict resolution strategies.

   _____   _____

   _____   _____

2. What are the four parts of the decision-making process?
   Step 1: _____
   Step 2: _____
   Step 3: _____
   Step 4: _____

3. What are the steps a peer mediator would use in a bullying situation?

    Step 1: _____

    Step 2: _____

    Step 3: _____

    Step 4: _____

    Step 5: _____

4. Name four positive ways you could express your anger.

    _____   _____

    _____   _____

5. What does it mean to respect someone? Name one way to show someone respect.

    _____

    _____

    _____

6. What are three things you could do if you were being bullied?

    _____

    _____

    _____

7. What are three things you could do if you see someone being bullied?

    _____

    _____

    _____

8. Name two ways you can help make our school a safer, friendlier place.

    _____

    _____

    _____

SUBUNIT ON PUBLIC POLICY

Created and Developed by Katie Ryan
Southwestern City Schools, Columbus, OH

CURRICULAR UNIT OUTCOMES:
CITIZENSHIP

Subunit One: Rights and Responsibilities

- Students will identify characteristics for obtaining American citizenship.
- Students will examine what it means to be an American citizen.
- Students will read and analyze the Constitution and the Bill of Rights to determine the rights, duties, and responsibilities of American citizens.
- Students will explore various democratic values, such as freedom, equality, and justice.
- Students will evaluate our society and the upholding of these values.
- Students will examine the ways people play the role of citizen and the effect they have on upholding democratic ideals.
- Students will define political efficacy and reflect upon their current role as a citizen.
- Students will develop a sense of political efficacy and describe ways to increase the efficacy of others.

Subunit Two: Levels of Government

- Students will define the various levels of government: federal, state, and local.
- Students will understand the defining characteristics, powers, and duties of each level of government.
- Students will be able to describe the relationship among local, state, and federal governments.
- Students will be able to distinguish the similarities and differences among the three levels.
- Students will analyze the need for balance among the national, state, and local governments.
- Students will identify ways in which citizens can influence all three levels of government.

Used with permission.

Subunit Three: Public Policy

- Students will define public policy, and be able to identify various examples of it. (knowledge, comprehension)
- Students will recognize the importance of monitoring policies and will demonstrate their ability to monitor policies through various avenues. (comprehension, application)
- Students will describe methods of influencing policies and analyze which methods are most effective at the various levels of government. (application, analysis)
- Students will identify problems at the local, state, and national level that need addressing. (comprehension)
- Students will identify a problem of their choice in their community to study. (application)
- Students will determine which level of government is directly responsible for dealing with this problem. (application)
- Students will research this problem, gathering and evaluating information about the problem from a variety of sources. (application, evaluation)
- Students will examine public policies that are currently being used by the government, and other agencies, and evaluate their effectiveness. (analysis, evaluation)
- Students will brainstorm and develop a creative solution to the problem by developing their own public policy. (synthesis)
- Students will develop an action plan on how to influence the appropriate government or agency to adopt their proposed policy. (synthesis)
- Students will actively become citizens by creating social action projects that allow them to actively influence public policy and problem solve. (synthesis)

PREASSESSMENT SURVEY: CITIZENSHIP ATTITUDES AND BELIEFS

Circle the letter that best describes how you feel about the sentence.

A = Agree   **D = Disagree**   **U = Unsure**

1. Teenagers should find ways to help others in the community.	A	D	U
2. I keep informed about the upcoming Presidential Election of 2004.	A	D	U
3. I feel that I can make a difference in my community.	A	D	U
4. Problems like pollution and poverty are not important to me.	A	D	U

5. Teenagers have a responsibility to do what they can   A   D   U
   to protect the environment.

6. I don't care about what is happening in politics.   A   D   U

7. Young people can influence public policies.   A   D   U

8. I read the newspaper or watch the news to keep   A   D   U
   up with what's happening in my community.

9. Other people's problems don't bother me.   A   D   U

10. I plan to vote when I am old enough.   A   D   U

11. What are some ways young people can influence society?

12. Do you vote in elections for student council?

13. Do you plan on monitoring or participating in the Presidential Election of
    2004? How so?

14. What are my responsibilities and duties as a young citizen in the USA?

15. How do you feel about the ability of the U.S. government to solve problems? Can young people help to solve society's problems?

LESSON: PUBLIC POLICY: WHAT IS IT?

Objective: Students will define public policy, and be able to identify
                       various examples of it.

Concepts/Skills: Develop characteristics of public policy, classification of
                       public policy into one of four categories: federal, state,
                       local, school

Materials: Examples of public policies (school code of conduct), traf-
                       fic laws (stop sign, etc.), poster paper, markers, transparency

Procedures:
Introductory Activity

- Prior to students entering the room, have many examples of public policy written on the board, or displayed in the front (examples include: school code of conduct, traffic laws [picture of stop sign], public smoking ban, music copyright laws, gun policies, drinking age, uniforms in schools).
- When students enter, ask them what do all of these items have in common? Brainstorm ideas on the board.
- Inform students that these are all public policies.
- Ask students what is a public policy?
- Create a graphic organizer (web diagram) on board.
- "Chalk Talk": Have a couple of students come to the board to extend the web, with what they already know or think they know about public policy; at the end of the lesson, they will add on to this web.

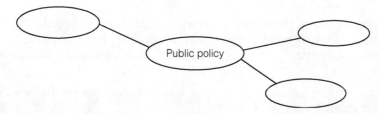

Developmental Activity

- Explain to students that they will be working in groups to investigate public policies and develop a definition (and characteristics) of public policies.
- Divide students into small groups of students (three or four students). Groups will be preassigned by me based on ability, so that each group contains students of diverse abilities. Also, each group member will be assigned a specific task, such as presenter, researcher, or recorder.
- Each group will be given a packet, which contains six different examples of public policies. For example, one packet might include a handout on the movie rating policy (G, PG, PG-13, and R-rated movies), food safety laws, seat belt laws, minimum wage law, school uniform policy, and public smoking ban policy. (Each group of students will receive a different packet.)
- Each group will be given a large piece of paper and markers.
- The group is to answer the following questions:
  - What are the similarities and differences between these public policies?
  - What would life be like, if we did not have these policies?
  - Create a list of characteristics of public policies and a definition of public policy
- Ask several groups to share their poster (their definitions and characteristics of public policy).

- Show students a transparency, which states the "official" definition of public policy. (*A public policy is an agreed upon way that our government, at whatever level, fulfills its responsibilities to protect individual rights and promote the common welfare. Some public policies are written into laws by legislatures, others are contained in rules and regulations created by executive branches of government—president, governor, mayor, school superintendent—the branches of government responsible for carrying out and enforcing laws.*)
- Ask students to recall the lessons on the various levels of government (from earlier in the unit), and have the students work as a group to classify the public policies in their handouts into the following categories: federal, state, local, and school policies.
- Ask some students to share their answers.

Concluding Activity

- Ask students to participate in "Chalk Talk" by having each student come up to the board and add onto the web diagram.
- Students should write one item they learned about public policy, whether it is a characteristic of public policies or an example. Students can also write a question on the web, which they are interested in learning the answer to.
- Ask students: What public policies affect your life on a regular basis? Why are public policies important?

Assessment:

For homework, students will come up with four examples of public policies, one from each category: federal, state, local, and school.

LESSON: IDENTIFYING PUBLIC POLICY PROBLEMS

Objective:	Students will identify problems at the local, state, and national level that need addressing.
	Students will determine which level of government is directly responsible for dealing with these problems.
Concepts/Skills:	Identification of problems at various government levels. Analysis and investigation of problems and public policies
Materials:	Handouts ("Problem Identification and Analysis Form" and "Common Problems in Communities"), books, newspaper articles, Internet (computers), journal articles.

Procedures:

Introductory Activity

- When students come in there will be a collage of newspaper articles on the board, which represent different problems at the local, state, and national levels. There may also be some example problems written on the board.

- When students are settled in, ask them what all the items on the board have in common. Listen to student answers. Guide them to realize that these are all problems that need to be changed through public policies.

- Ask students to identify additional public policy problems that can be added to the collage on the board. Ask them to identify some problems that are specific to young people their age and problems in schools.

Developmental Activity

- Explain to students that they will be working in groups of two or three students.

- Students may work with peers of their choice from their table clusters (which are already preassigned).

- Each group will receive a packet with two handouts: "Problem Identification and Analysis" and "Common Problems in Communities." Each group is to read the example problems in the "Common Problems in Communities" handout. Students should brainstorm some additional problems and add them to the sheet.

- Each group should then choose one problem to investigate and analyze. (Students can also get ideas from the collage on the board.) Tell students that they will be presenting their findings to the rest of the class at the end of the period.

- Each group should discuss and investigate this problem using the handout "Problem Identification." Students can use resources in the room (newspaper articles, books, or the Internet) to help them with this. Students will analyze the effectiveness of the public policies in place to deal with this problem.

- Sample questions on the handout: Is this a problem that you and other people in your community think is important? Why? What policy, if any, does government have to deal with this problem? If a policy does exist, does this policy need to be replaced? Why?

- Each group will identify which level of government and/or which agency is responsible for dealing with this problem.

- Each group will share their problem, what they learned, and their findings from their answers on their handout with the class. Students can present orally or create a graphic organizer or poster to aid in their presentation.

Concluding Activity:

- Have students add their problems to the collage on the board—by adding their posters, or by writing their ideas on the board.

- Ask students to classify problems on the board (newspaper collage). Pick several out from the board and ask students: Are these problems dealt with at the local, state, or national level? (checking their comprehension and retention from material learned today and in the government unit)

- Ask students what did we learn today? Review: We identified problems in our community, state, or country, and analyzed public policies. Ask: What challenges does our government face in addressing and solving these problems?

- Inform students briefly that, in the near future, the class will be investigating and learning about methods of change and solving problems. Tell them that as a class, we will be exploring issues that we personally want to address. We will become active citizens. Students will be selecting a problem to study as a small group and developing a social action plan to solve it.

- Explain homework assignment.

Assessment: Homework Assignment

Students are to find out more about the problem they identified today. They have one of three options. Choose one!

1. They can bring in a newspaper article or another print source that details more information about their problem. They will answer questions about their source. They will fill out the "Printed Source" handout.

2. They can interview a family, friend, or community member to see what they know about the problem or how they feel about it. They will fill out the "Interview Form" handout.

3. They can listen to a news report on the radio or TV for information concerning their problem. They will fill out the "Observation Form" handout with information about their problem.

Problem Identification and Analysis Form

Names of group members _____

Date _____

The problem_____

1. Is this a problem that you and other people in your community think is important? Why?

   _____

   _____

2. What level of government or governmental agency is responsible for dealing with the problem?

   _____

   _____

3. What policy, if any, does government now have to deal with this problem?

_____

_____

If a policy does exist, answer the following questions:

What are its advantages and disadvantages? _____

_____

_____

How might it be improved? _____

_____

_____

Does this policy need to be replaced? Why? _____

_____

_____

What disagreements, if any, exist in your community about this policy?

_____

_____

4. Where can you get more information about this problem and the positions taken by different individuals and groups?

_____

_____

_____

5. Are there other problems in your community that you think might be useful for your class to study? What are they?

_____

_____

_____

_____

Common Problems in Communities

Communities across the United States have many problems in common. Some problems may be more serious in some communities than in others. People often think that government should be responsible for adopting policies to help solve these problems.

Problems in Schools

- Many people claim that schools do not teach skills that adequately prepare students to get jobs when they graduate.
- Some students use language and other forms of expression that are insulting to certain groups.
- Gang activity both in and out of school makes many students afraid for their personal safety.

Problems Regarding Young People

- Young people sometimes work long hours in after school or weekend jobs. This often makes it difficult for them to do well in school.
- Some working parents do not have enough money to pay for adequate care for their children during work hours. As a result, young children may be left home alone, sometimes in dangerous circumstances.

Problems Involving Basic Liberties

- Large numbers of people do not vote in elections. This is especially true in local elections.
- Many people argue that money plays too great a role in the election of government officials.

Problems Concerning the Environment

- Some communities do not have recycling programs, or those they have do not work well.
- Some communities have industries that pollute into rivers and lakes.

List some additional problems:

_____

LESSON: PARTICIPATING IN AND INFLUENCING PUBLIC POLICY

Objective: Students will describe methods of influencing policies and analyze which methods are most effective at various levels of government.

Concepts/Skills: Students will analyze advantages and disadvantages of various methods of influencing policies. Students will present their ideas to the class and share a way in which people can influence their public policy problem.

Materials: PowerPoint presentation (laptop and projector), paper, markers

Procedures:

Introductory Activity

- When students come into class, ask them how many voted in the last school election. Why? How do citizens participate in our government?
- Inform them that today we will be learning how people can participate in and influence public policies.

Developmental Activity

- Show students a PowerPoint presentation of ways people participate in and influence public policy.
- Examples that will be included are: people voting in various elections, participating in political discussions, signing of petitions, writing letters to elected representatives, attending meetings to discuss issues or lend support, campaigning for a candidate, running for office, contributing money to a party, lobbying for special interest laws, and trying to persuade people to vote, or to vote a certain way.
- Have students work with a partner or in a small group (the same group for lesson 2, in which they investigated a public policy problem).
- Students will develop a list on big paper and post in the room. Students will list advantages and disadvantages of each form of participation.
- Ask students: Are all these forms of participation and influencing equally important in protecting our basic rights? Why or why not? Which seem the most important? Which forms of influencing public policies would you use at each level of government? Do specific forms of participation or influencing lend themselves to specific levels of government?
- Have each group revisit the public policy problem that they have recently been investigating.
- Students will select a method of how they could influence this public policy problem they have been studying. Then the students will present this method to the class either through a cartoon, role playing, or poster presentation.

Closure

- Write on the board: How satisfied are you with our government? Have students pick a number between 1 and 10 to describe their level of satisfaction and explain their answer by listing five things that support their level of satisfaction or dissatisfaction.
- Have several students share their rating and justification.
- Ask students: What are some ways we can influence changes in our government to increase our satisfaction? For those who rated a high satisfaction with government: How is public policy related to this? What are some effective public policies that our government implements?

Assessment:
Ask students to briefly respond to the following question: Should students influence public policies and participate in government? How can students do this?

LESSON: SELECTING A PROBLEM FOR CLASS SOCIAL ACTION PROJECTS

Objective: Students will identify a problem of their choice in their community to study. Students will determine which level of government is directly responsible for dealing with this problem. Students will research this problem, gathering and evaluating information about the problem from a variety of sources.

Concepts/Skills: Identification of problem, research skills, working with other people in a group

Materials: handouts in folders (project packet), photos, maps, computers, resources

Duration: This lesson may take a couple of days. Day 1 is primarily an introduction to the project, and the identification of the problem to study. Day 2 is to start research. (Future lessons will include minilessons and time for research as well.)

Procedures:
Introductory Activity

- When students enter the classroom, there will be photos and maps of the area community (city or town in which they live) and also of the state. There will also be some community problems written on the board that the students have been learning about, such as pollution and vandalism.
- Ask students to list other problems that we find in our community—local, state, or even national.
- Teacher will inform students that today we will be starting a social action project, in which we will work in teams of four students to identify a community problem to study in depth, research, and develop a public policy of our own to solve the problem.

Developmental Activity

- Divide students into their Social Action Team. Each group will have four students. The students are preassigned by me based on different needs and abilities so that each group has a variety of students who can work cooperatively together.

- Inform each group that they will need to come up with a team name by the end of the period—for example, The Star Citizens.

- Pass out "Social Action Project Overview" packet (folders). This packet gives an introduction and overview of the project purpose and requirements. There is a step-by-step guide to the process: Students will identify a problem to study, gather information (research), examine public policies now in place, develop their own public policy, and develop an action plan. Checklists and rubrics are also included.

- Go over the purpose of the project and over the steps and requirements discussed in the packet. Ask students for questions. Does anything need to be clarified?

- Instruct students to work in their group, to choose one problem they will study as a team in depth. Each student may give a suggestion and a justification on why they want to study that problem. Students can then decide together what their problem will be. Questions to consider when deciding are: Why is this problem important? What people does it affect? What kind of impact does it have on the community? (These questions will be written on the board.) Once the students decide, they must inform the teacher of their chosen problem.

- Students will record their chosen problem on the "Problem Identification" handout.

- Students will then determine which level of government or government agency they believe is responsible for dealing with this problem.

(Depending on Time)

Closure

- Now that students have their problem identified, ask students: How do you think you might go about researching this problem? What sources might you use?

- Tell them to start thinking about this.

Assessment:
Students should bring in one source or idea for a source that they can research for the next class.

Day 2
Introductory Activity

- Have each group present their new team name and share the problem they will be studying.

- Ask each group to add their problem to the board (yesterday's materials and writings about community problems will still be present).

- Ask students: How can we learn more about our problem?

Developmental Activity

- Teacher will lead a minilesson on research. Teacher will inform students that before we start researching as a team, we will be doing a minireview of good research sources.

- Teacher will ask for 10 volunteers. Teacher will pass out 10 slips of paper, one slip to each student. Each slip contains a source of information. Examples include: newspaper article, interview with a lawyer, government web site, evening TV news.

- Students will be instructed to arrange themselves in a line—a continuum from least appropriate (least reliable/valid) source to most appropriate/reliable source.

- Teacher will lead a class discussion, in which the students decide if the students are arranged in the line appropriately. The class will then rearrange the line until they find the continuum that is most appropriate. The teacher will then discuss the importance of using good sources, and finding the same information in more than one source.

- Teacher will then direct the students that they will be conducting research in their teams.

- Students will follow the section in their project folders about research. They will look at the list of suggested sources (such as newspapers, school library book and journals, interviews with professionals, or government agencies.) Students will brainstorm in their team some other sources of where they might get information. They will record these.

- The students will work together to devise a research plan (found in packet).

- The students will divide up how they will obtain and document the information.

- For example, one student may decide he will visit the library, while another student may call an office on the phone, someone else may arrange to interview a community member, and someone else may e-mail an official or government representative and ask for more information.

- Students will then have the remainder of class to research using computers in the classroom or computer lab, or go to the school library.

Closure

- Ask students: Where did you find your information today?
- What sources will you be using?
- Make a list on the board. (Or have one member from each group come up and write a source.) This way, other class members may get some ideas.

- Finally, ask students: How does researching this community problem affect us? What will this mean for our community?

Assessment:
Have each team (two per student) bring in eight sources by the end of the week, with a summary of the information found in their source. (Fill out proper sheet in the packet "What I Found Out About My Problem.")

POSTASSESSMENT

Upon completion of the social action projects, these will be evaluated as the unit postassessment. The social action projects allow students to identify a problem in their community to study, research the problem, examine current public policies and analyze their effectiveness, develop their own public policy, and develop an action plan on how to influence the government and adopt the new proposed policy. The students will have a project presentation day, where they present their social action projects to the class and invited community members. Students will also turn in a portfolio of their team's work. Finally, students will write a short reflection paper on what they have learned from this experience. This project allows students to become active citizens, and hence, it is an appropriate assessment for this unit.

Some of the ways that the presentations and portfolios will be assessed are (rubrics and checklists will be used):

Criteria:

Completeness—all sections are complete

Clarity, organization—easy to understand

Information—research

Support—examples, explanations

Graphics—do they convey information or support it?

Documentation—reliable/valid sources and information

Constitutionality—how your policy fits within the constitution (doesn't violate it)

Persuasiveness—can convince others this is a good idea/project/solution to problem

Practicality—realistic

Coordination—portfolio and presentation coordinate with one another

Reflection—demonstrate that you have learned from this experience

POSTASSESSMENT SURVEY:
CITIZENSHIP ATTITUDES AND BELIEFS

Circle the letter that best describes how you feel about the sentence.

A = Agree   **D = Disagree**   **U = Unsure**

1. Teenagers should find ways to help others in the community.   A   D   U

2. I keep informed about the upcoming Presidential Election.   A   D   U

3. I feel that I can make a difference in my community.   A   D   U

4. Problems like pollution and poverty are not important to me.   A   D   U

5. Teenagers have a responsibility to do what they can to protect the environment.   A   D   U

6. I don't care about what is happening in politics.   A   D   U

7. Young people can influence public policies.   A   D   U

8. I read the newspaper or watch the news to keep up with what's happening in my community.   A   D   U

9. Other people's problems don't bother me.   A   D   U

10. I plan to vote when I am old enough.   A   D   U

11. What are some ways young people can influence society?

12. Do you vote in elections for student council?

13. Do you plan on monitoring or participating in the Presidential Election? How so?

14. What are my responsibilities and duties as a young citizen in the USA?

15. How do you feel about the ability of the U.S. government to solve problems? Can young people help to solve society's problems?

INSTRUCTIONAL DESIGN

Forensic Science: Sample Lessons

Created and Developed by Nathan Ash
Van Buren (OH) High School

UNIT INTENDED LEARNING OUTCOMES

Forensic Science

- Students will be able to define forensic science and describe situations where forensic science can be used. (knowledge)
- Students will gather, analyze, and summarize evidence from the perspective of a forensic examiner. (application, analysis)
- Students will define chromatography. (knowledge)
- Students will explain how pigments are separated through capillary action. (comprehension)
- Students will demonstrate the ability to make chromatograms from known samples as well as collected evidence using proper laboratory techniques. (application)
- Students will analyze chromatograms for comparison with evidence. (evaluation)
- Students will demonstrate that they can set up fields in a database. (application)
- Students will construct a database using fields that they feel are integral in a descriptive record. (synthesis)
- Students will manage the database: entering data, sorting data, and searching for entries. (application)
- Students will demonstrate skills used to examine sample fibers through a microscope. (application)
- Students will identify visible characteristics of fibers under magnification. (analysis)
- Students will perform flame tests to identify chemical properties of heat resistance, flammability, and odor. (application)
- Students will classify fibers and compare to known fibers. (comprehension)
- Students will define the major fingerprint ridge patterns as whorls, loops, and arches. (knowledge)
- Students will identify the major patterns in fingerprint ridges such as whorls, loops, and arches for a fingerprint sample. (knowledge)

- Students will be able to collect fingerprints from suspects by using graphite and clear tape. (application)
- Students will isolate and identify ridge characteristics (hooks, eyes, end ridges, forks, etc.) on collected fingerprints. (analysis)
- Students will explain how characteristics of fingerprints can be used as forensic evidence. (comprehension)
- Students will use characteristics of the ridge patterns to match fingerprints. (evaluation)
- Students will use forensic evidence to argue a case against a suspect. (evaluation)

FORENSIC SCIENCE: CONCEPT CHECK AND ASSESSMENT

Name: _____

Instructions: Before learning, rate yourself on the left with a plus (+) if you are an expert, a check (✓) if you know a little about it, and a zero (0) if the term is new to you. After the learning experience, you can again evaluate yourself on these terms by using the spaces on the right side.

Before Learning	Concept or Terms	After Learning
_____	Forensic science	_____
_____	Fibers	_____
_____	Pliability	_____
_____	Hair analysis	_____
_____	Casting	_____
_____	Forensic evidence	_____
_____	Fingerprint	_____
_____	Whorl	_____
_____	Ridge pattern	_____
_____	Latent prints	_____
_____	Database	_____
_____	Chromatography	_____
_____	Capillary action	_____
_____	DNA	_____
_____	DNA fingerprinting	_____
_____	Blood typing	_____
_____	Crime scene	_____
_____	Chain of custody	_____

Forensic Science Unit: 11th–12th Benchmarks

Rating Key: 3—high correlation 2—good correlation 1—weak correlation 0—no correlation

Forensic Science Lessons →	Setting up notebook	Background research	Chem & Phys prop. of hair	Hair analysis	Shoe prints	Fingerprinting	Writing analysis	Surface chro-matography	Blood typing	Creating a database	Mapping a crime scene	Final crime scene
PHYSICAL SCIENCE												
A. Explain how variations in the arrangement and motion of atoms and molecules form the basis of a variety of biological, chemical and physical phenomena.	0	0	1	0	0	0	0	2	2	0	0	2
B. Recognize that some atomic nuclei are unstable and will spontaneously break down.	0	0	0	0	0	0	0	0	0	0	0	0
C. Describe how atoms and molecules can gain or lose energy only in discrete amounts.	0	0	0	0	0	0	0	0	0	0	0	0
D. Apply principles of forces and motion to mathematically analyze, describe and predict the net effects on objects or systems.	0	0	0	0	0	0	0	0	0	0	0	0
E. Summarize the historical development of scientific theories and ideas within the study of physical sciences.	0	0	0	0	0	2	0	0	0	0	0	1
SCIENCE & TECHNOLOGY												
A. Predict how human choices today will determine the quality and quantity of life on Earth.	0	2	0	0	0	1	0	0	0	0	0	2

Forensic Science Unit: 11th–12th Benchmarks

Rating Key: 3—high correlation   2—good correlation   1—weak correlation   0—no correlation

Forensic Science Lessons →	Setting up notebook	Background research	Chem & Phys prop. of hair	Hair analysis	Shoe prints	Fingerprinting	Writing analysis	Surface chromatography	Blood typing	Creating a database	Mapping a crime scene	Final crime scene
SCIENTIFIC INQUIRY												
A. Make appropriate choices when designing and participating in scientific investigations by using cognitive and manipulative skills when collecting data and formulating conclusions from the data.	3	3	3	3	3	3	3	3	3	1	3	3
SCIENTIFIC WAYS OF KNOWING												
A. Explain how scientific evidence is used to develop and revise scientific predictions, ideas or theories.	0	3	2	2	2	2	2	2	2	0	2	3
B. Explain how ethical considerations shape scientific endeavors.	0	3	0	0	0	1	0	0	1	0	0	3
C. Explain how societal issues and considerations affect the progress of science and technology.	0	3	1	1	1	3	1	1	2	0	0	3

5 E'S LESSON PLAN FOR SCIENCE

Theme: *Forensic Science: Surface Chromatography*	

Science Benchmarks: Physical Science 11-12: A, Science & Technology 11-12: none Scientific Inquiry 11-12: A Scientific Ways of Knowing 11-12: A,C [*Note:* Letters in benchmarks refer to standards in the district curriculum guide.]	**Objectives:** ■ Students will define chromatography. ■ Students will explain how pigments are separated through capillary action. ■ Students will demonstrate the ability to make chromatograms from known samples as well as collected evidence using proper laboratory techniques. ■ Students will analyze chromatograms for comparison purposes.
Time Requirements: two days *Needed Lab Materials or Technology* Chromatography paper, pencils, felt-tip pens (various colors), test tubes, forceps, straightened paper clips, DI water, ethanol solution, goggles	**Concepts/Skills:** ■ Chromatography and comparison of chromatograms ■ Capillary action ■ Establishing empirical standards ■ Measurement techniques ■ Proper safety considerations and laboratory techniques
How I will **ENGAGE** the students using connections to their prior knowledge.	Day 1: Use an imaginary note from the office to show as evidence of forgery. Explain how ink on paper can be analyzed to see what kind of device was used to write with. Also, read out loud the "Science Connections" in *Science in a Technical World: Forensic Science* on page 47.
What students will do to **EXPLORE** the concepts and begin to develop vocabulary at the same time.	Day 1: Follow Laboratory 5 in *Science in a Technical World: Forensic Science*, pp. 44–48. The students will do chromatography of different known inks with different mobile phases. The capillary rise of the mobile phase will take the rest of the period into the next day.
What I will do to allow students an opportunity to construct their own **EXPLANATION** of the concepts.	Day 2: In their journals, students will answer the "Analyzing the Data Questions" in *Science in a Technical World: Forensic Science* on page 48.
Opportunities I will give students to **ELABORATE** or extend their understanding of the concepts.	Day 2: Students will use collected evidence (from a handwritten note) and perform a surface chromatography to determine which pen was used to write the note.

How I and/or the student will **EVALUATE** his or her learning.	Day 2 for homework: The students will answer the following questions to be turned in: a. When comparing the evidence writing sample to the standard, why is it important to use the same kind of solvent that was used for setting up the standard? b. Can chromatography yield useful evidence, even if the name and exact composition of the ink is not known? Explain. c. What are some mixtures other than ink that might be separated by chromatography? (*Science in a Technical World: Forensic Science,* p. 48.)
Teacher Notes:	

5 E'S LESSON PLAN FOR SCIENCE

Theme: *Forensic Science: Creating and Using a Database*

Science Benchmarks:	**Objectives:**
Physical Science 11–12: none Science & Technology 11–12: A Scientific Inquiry 11–12: A Scientific Ways of Knowing 11–12: A, B, C	■ Students will demonstrate that they can set up fields in a database. ■ Students will construct a database using fields that they feel are integral in a descriptive record. ■ Students will manage the database: entering data, sorting data, and searching for entries.
Time Requirements: 4 days *Needed Lab Materials or Technology* student CD's (5 different types), computers with Microsoft Access database software	**Concepts/Skills:** ■ Using the computers to make a database in Microsoft Access ■ Techniques to sort, filter, and search in a database
How I will **ENGAGE** the students using connections to their prior knowledge.	Day 1: Encourage students to bring CD's a music that show the spectrum of their musical interests. Explain that we are going to make a class-wide database that holds all of the class's information.
What students will do to **EXPLORE** the concepts and begin to develop vocabulary at the same time.	Day 1: Students will begin to work with Access to figure out how to make a database formats. They will also determine what values are important to be used as fields in the database. Day 2: Students will create a music database and begin entering the information from their CDs—this information will be compiled by the teacher after all values have been entered.
What I will do to allow students an opportunity to construct their own **EXPLANATION** of the concepts.	Day 3: Students will write an essay of how a database works and what kind of data should be considered for a useful database.
Opportunities I will give students to **ELABORATE** or extend their understanding of the concepts.	Day 3: The different groups of students will generate questions about the classroom music database for other groups to sort, filter, and search for.

How I and/or the student will **EVALUATE** his or her learning.	Day 4: Each group will discuss what fields may be important in a suspect database, then the group will create a database format for later use in the unit.
Teacher Notes:	

5 E'S LESSON PLAN FOR SCIENCE

Theme *Forensic Science: Fibers*	
Science Benchmarks: Physical Science 11–12: none Science & Technology 11–12: none Scientific Inquiry 11–12: A Scientific Ways of Knowing 11–12: A, C	**Objectives:** ■ Students will demonstrate skills used to examine sample fibers through a microscope. ■ Students will identify visible characteristics of fibers under magnification. ■ Students will perform flame tests to identify chemical properties of heat resistance, flammability, and odor. ■ Students will classify fibers and compare to known fibers.
Time Requirements: two days *Needed Lab Materials or Technology* Per group: aprons, gloves, labeled sample fibers, unknown fiber sample, microscope (optional digital), forceps, slide and cover slips, tap water, dropper	**Concepts/Skills:** ■ Observe and follow forensic laboratory procedures and follow safety precautions ■ Characterization of fibers through observations ■ Use of dissecting microscope ■ Proper use of Bunsen burner
How I will **ENGAGE** the students using connections to their prior knowledge.	Day 1: Have students pull fibers from their shirts or sweaters and then draw in their journals what they think the fiber will look like under magnification. Day 2: Discuss how fibers might be used as forensic evidence.
What students will do to **EXPLORE** the concepts and begin to develop vocabulary at the same time.	Day 1: ■ Students will collect the different fiber samples and make tables that organize the information they are about to collect (*Science in a Technical World: Forensic Science*, p. 19). ■ Students will test and observe the properties of texture, color, crimp, pliability, and resilience. They will also will observe the fiber under 10X magnification and draw a sketch. Day 2: ■ Students will use a Bunsen burner to test fibers near the flame. ■ Students will use a Bunsen burner to test fibers in a flame. (*Science in a Technical World: Forensic Science*, pp. 22–24.)

What I will do to allow students an opportunity to construct their own **EXPLANATION** of the concepts.	Day 1: In their journals, students will answer *Analyzing Data* questions in the book about properties of fibers (*Science in a Technical World: Forensic Science,* p. 21). Day 2: In their journals, students will answer *Analyzing Data* questions in the book about the distinctions between manmade and natural fibers (*Science in a Technical World: Forensic Science,* p. 24).
Opportunities I will give students to **ELABO-RATE** or extend their understanding of the concepts.	■ Have small group discussion: Is it possible to have two samples that are the same type of fiber but do not match? Explain your answer. ■ How could a forensic scientist use these tests to help solve a case? (*Science in a Technical World: Forensic Science,* p. 21.)
How I and/or the student will **EVALUATE** his/her learning.	■ Give the students an unknown fiber type and match it to one of the fibers they have investigated. The students will record observations and test procedures that show the foundations of their conclusions.
Teacher Notes:	

5 E'S LESSON PLAN FOR SCIENCE

Theme *Forensic Science: Fingerprint Analysis*	
Science Benchmarks: Physical Science 11–12: E Science & Technology 11–12: A Scientific Inquiry 11–12: A Scientific Ways of Knowing 11–12: A, B, C	**Objectives:** ■ Students will define the major fingerprint ridge patterns as whorls, loops, and arches. ■ Students will identify the major patterns in fingerprint ridges such as whorls, loops, and arches for a fingerprint sample. ■ Students will be able to collect fingerprints from suspects by using graphite and clear tape.
Time Requirements: two days *Needed Lab Materials or Technology* Graphite pencils, note cards, wide clear tape, hand lens	**Concepts/Skills:** ■ Make fingerprints with graphite and clear tape ■ Characterizing ridge patterns of fingerprints ■ Using handheld magnifying lenses
How I will **ENGAGE** the students using connections to their prior knowledge.	Day 1: Show a clip of *CSI* "Scuba Doobie Doo" about how fingerprints are collected and analyzed.
What students will do to **EXPLORE** the concepts and begin to develop vocabulary at the same time.	Day 1: Laboratory 4, Part A of *Science in a Technical World: Forensic Science*, pp. 35–38, the students will read background information about fingerprints and then make their own fingerprints with graphite. These fingerprints will be used later on in the assessment of the unit.
What I will do to allow students an opportunity to construct their own **EXPLANATION** of the concepts.	Day 1 : With their own fingerprints, the students will identify which ridge pattern their fingerprints are.
Opportunities I will give students to **ELABO-RATE** or extend their understanding of the concepts.	Day 2: The class will tally all of the different ridge patterns for the entire class and come of with a relative percentage of each pattern.

How I and/or the student will **EVALUATE** his or her learning.	Day 2: There will be small group discussions about the fingerprinting techniques used. They will answer the questions: a. What is the most common ridge pattern in class? b. How can the information of the percentage of ridge patterns in this class be used to help narrow suspects down? c. Does our class distributions of ridge patterns agree with the national percentages that are given by the FBI? Explain the differences if there are any. (*Science in a Technical World: Forensic Science*, p. 38.)
Teacher Notes:	

5 E'S LESSON PLAN FOR SCIENCE

Theme *Forensic Science: Fingerprint Matching*

Science Benchmarks:	**Objectives:**
Physical Science 11–12: E Science & Technology 11–12: A Scientific Inquiry 11–12: A Scientific Ways of Knowing 11–12: A, B, C	■ Students will isolate and identify ridge characteristics (hooks, eyes, end ridges, forks, etc.) on collected fingerprints. ■ Students will explain how characteristics of fingerprints can be used as forensic evidence. ■ Students will use characteristics of the ridge patterns to match fingerprints.
Time Requirements : two days *Needed Lab Materials or Technology* Graphite pencils, notecards, wide clear tape, hand lens, NEO Science kit "Forensic Science" fingerprint packet	**Concepts/Skills:** ■ Identifying ridge characteristics ■ Comparison of fingerprints for characteristics and features ■ Using handheld magnifying lenses

How I will **ENGAGE** the students using connections to their prior knowledge.	Day 1: Read a story of a real crime and tell the students that a fingerprint has been recovered from the crime scene. They are going to investigate the procedures used to collect, analyze, and match latent fingerprints to suspects' fingerprints.
What students will do to **EXPLORE** the concepts and begin to develop vocabulary at the same time.	Day 1: Students will be given a fingerprint pack from Flinn Scientific kit *Flinn Fingerprinting Kit.* Students will study the characteristics and ridge patterns of the fingerprints in the packet.
What I will do to allow students an opportunity to construct their own **EXPLANATION** of the concepts.	Day 1: Students will use the Flinn kit packet as well as the NEO Science *Detective's Casebook Investigation Kit,* pp. 12–15, to study the fingerprints and circle identifiable characteristics of the fingerprints and label them correctly (i.e., hook, eye, end ridge, etc.).
Opportunities I will give students to **ELABO-RATE** or extend their understanding of the concepts.	Day 2: The students should explain in a focused freewrite how the identification of a suspect's fingerprints is accomplished through the use of the characteristics circled in their packets. They should relate this knowledge with the episode of *CSI* that we watched as a class, showing the similarities and differences in the way that we can match fingerprints in the class and how *CSI* scientists match fingerprints.

How I and/or the student will **EVALUATE** his or her learning.	Day 2: A handout of enlarged fingerprint will be given to the students and they must identify the ridge pattern type and circle at least five ridge pattern characteristics and identify them.
Teacher Notes:	

Websites
for Discipline-Based
Learned Societies

National Council for Teachers of Mathematics (NCTM)	http://www.nctm.org/
National Science Teachers Association (NSTA)	http://www.nsta.org/
National Council for Social Studies (NCSS)	http://www.ncss.org/
National Council of Teachers of English (NCTE)	http://ncte.org/
International Reading Association (IRA)	http://ira.org/
National Association for the Education of Young Children (NAEYC)	http://naeyc.org/
National Middle School Association (NMSA)	http://nmsa.org

Name Index

Subject Index

CPSIA information can be obtained
at www.ICGtesting.com
Printed in the USA
FFHW010020270319
51284414-56770FF